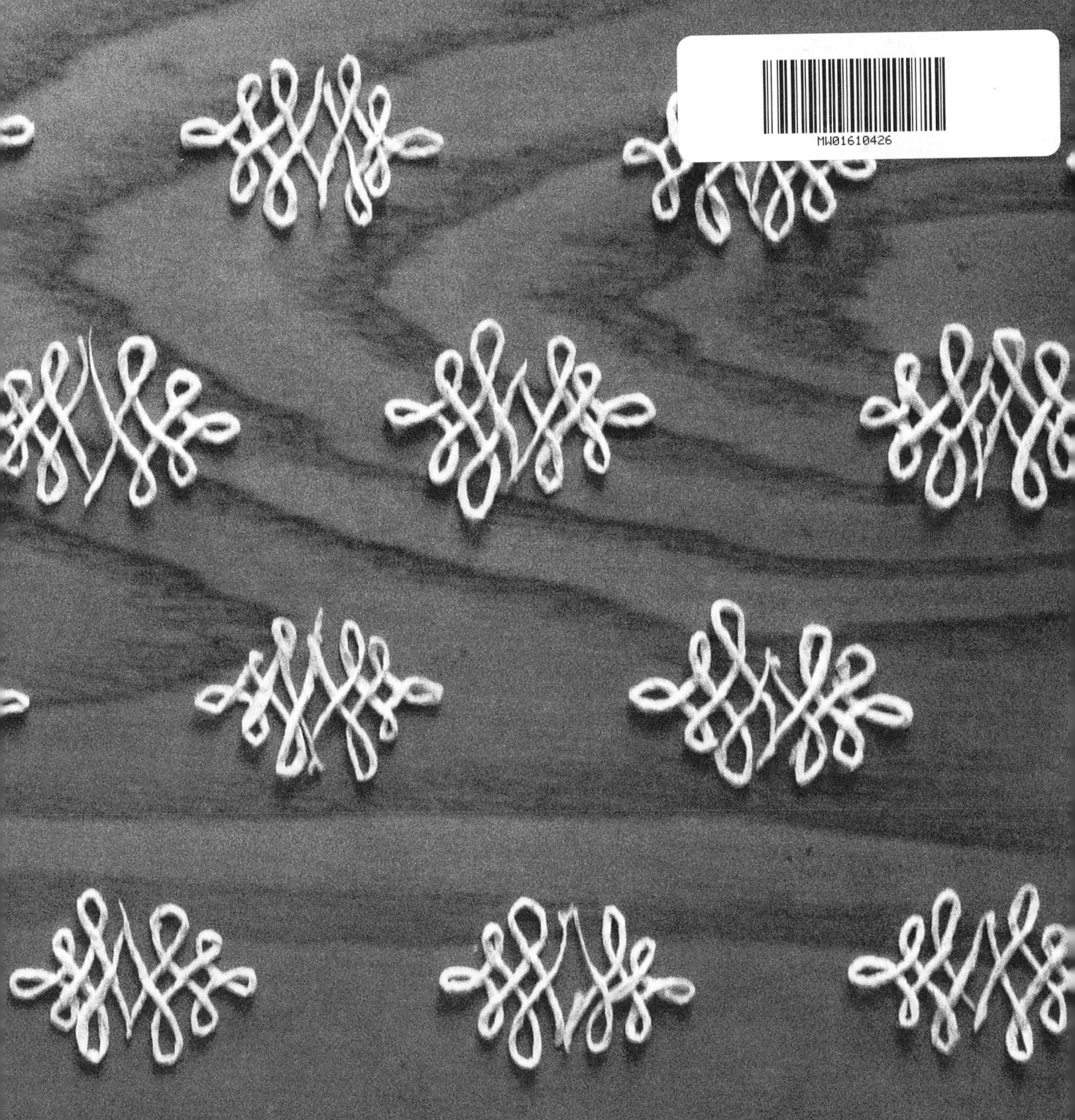

For Mom and Dad and Barry

Playing with Napkins, Volume 1

© 2014 by Brian D. Parker

Published by
Far Reach Publishing
Nashville, Tennessee

Book design and artwork by Brian D. Parker

Layout by Priceless Digital Media

Photography by Barry A. Noland, Brian D. Parker

Editing by F. Lynne Bachleda, Barry A. Noland

Photo editing by Ned Robertson

ISBN-10: 0-692-30445-2
ISBN-13: 978-0-692-30445-7

PLAYING WITH NAPKINS

Temporary Artworks from Coffee Shop Detritus
by
Brian D. Parker

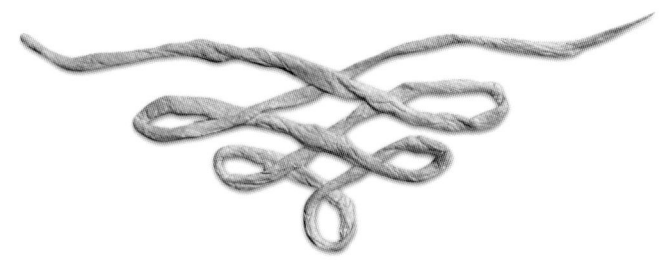

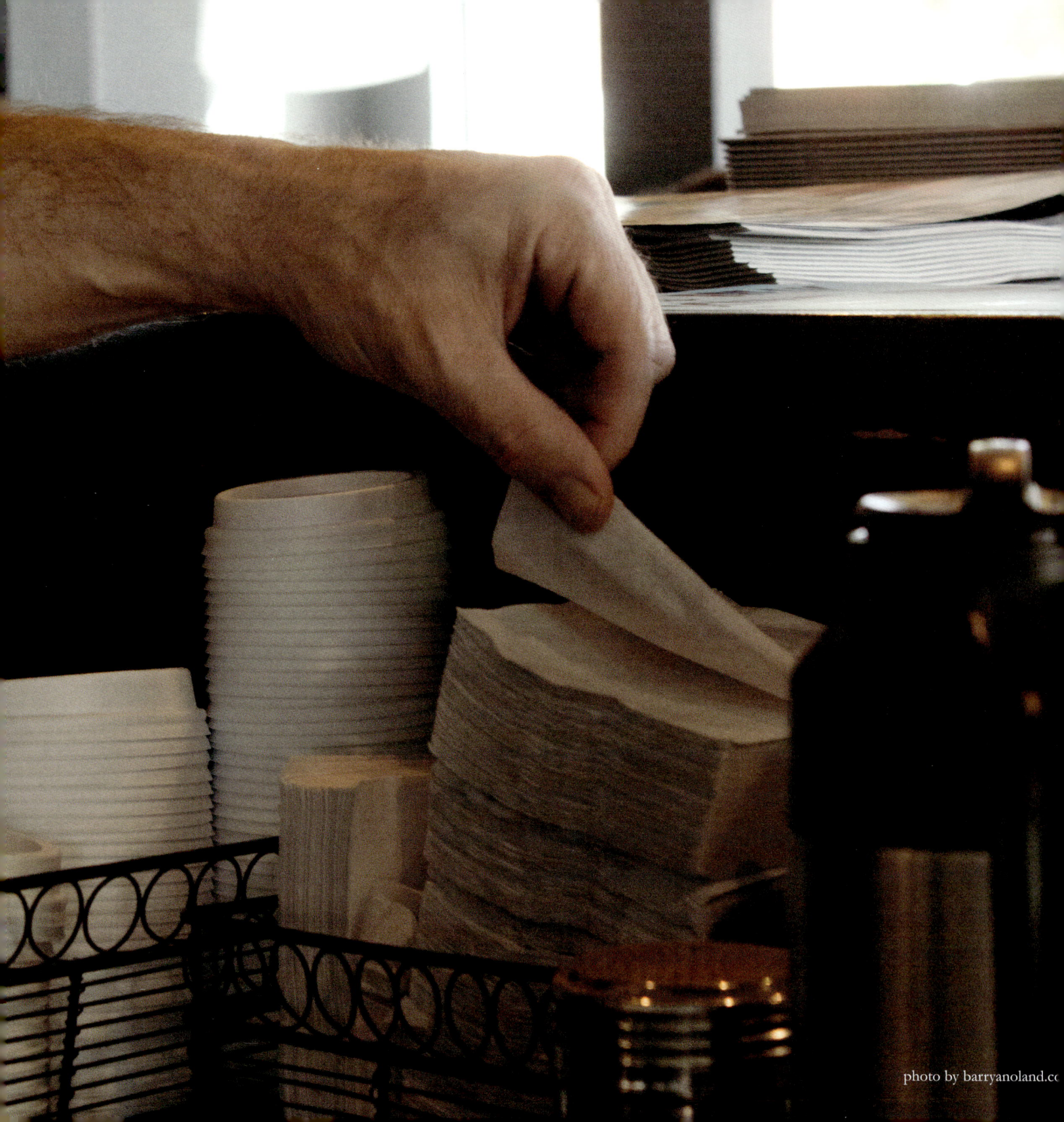

TABLE OF CONTENTS

Cortado   3.50
latte   3.50 3.75 4.00
flav. latte   3.75 4.00 4.25
mocha   4.00 4.25 4.50
americano   2.75 3.00 3.25
extra shot/
  non-dairy   .75

Roasted Chestnut
Tea Latte

• The Hayride   Montana Gold tea
                 steeped in local apple
                 cider

• Pumpkin Latte

Still available:

The Hoodie   The Black Bear
                 the Coleman

ALL PRICES INCLUDE TAX ☺

drip coffee   1.85 2.00 2.
iced coffee
vietnamese   3.25 3.
                       4.00

TEA & MORE

hot tea   2.75
iced tea   3.00
chai   4.00 4.25
hot chocolate   3.25 3.50
italian soda
cremosa

d Brew Menu

Kaldi Coffee
        Roasting Co St Louis Mo

uatemala Santiago de Atitlan
Tastes like: Concord grape, molasses, cocoa

umatra Lintong (wet hulled)
Tastes like: vanilla, butterscotch

Mexico Coatepec
Tastes like: strawberry, citrus

SOLD OUT

ICED TEAS:

• Minnesota
  N'ice (Black)
• Green Mango

• Peppermint
           (herbal)

Apple
Galette $3.50

BROWN SUGAR
SHORTBREAD
$3.50

Zucchini
Bran muffin
$2.75

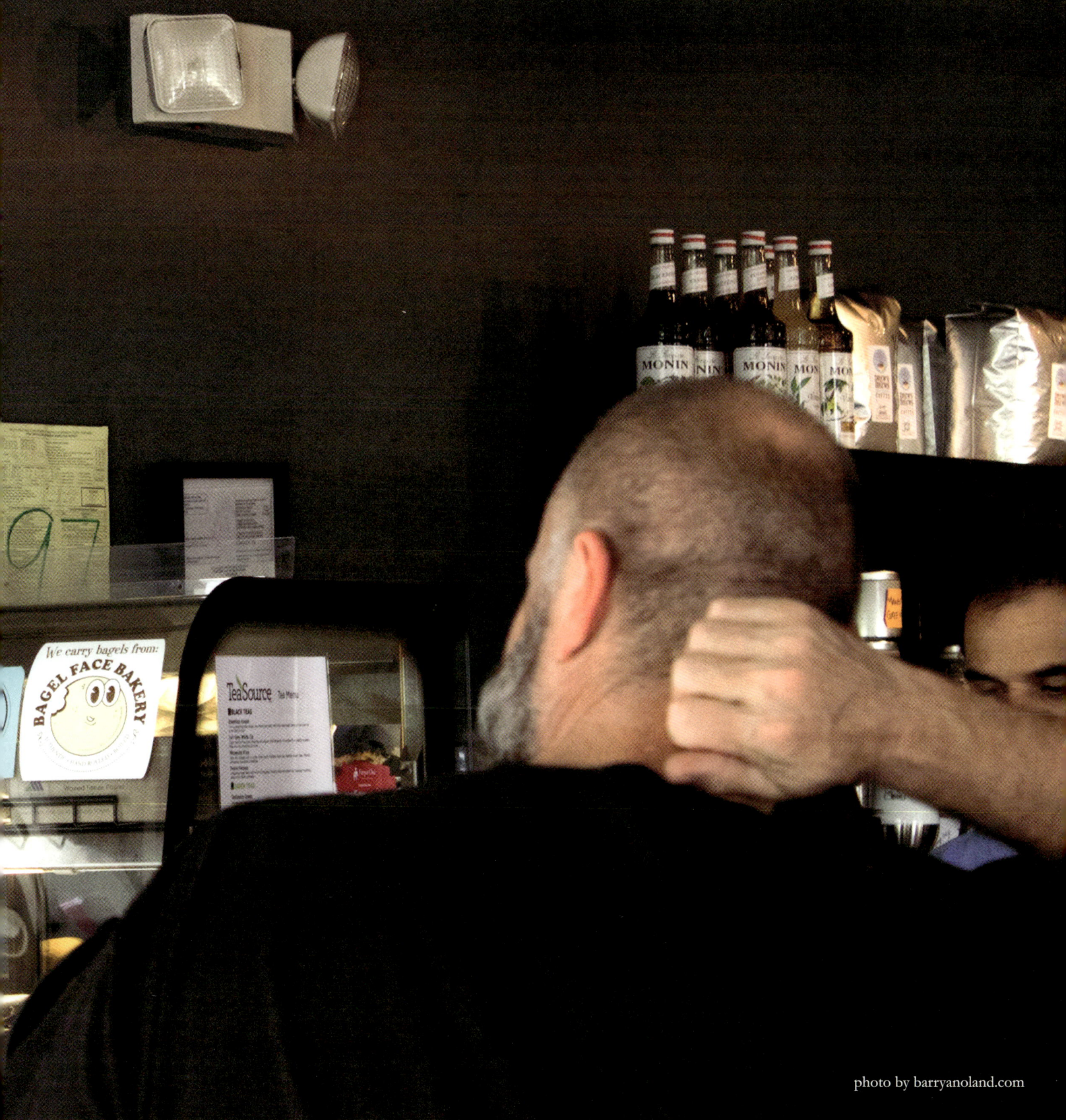

THE NAPKIN PROCESS

Most of the artworks were created at Ugly Mugs on a Sunday morning using only one or two napkins, spoons and sweetener packets — items that come wtih coffee and a bagel. You will also see plastic wrap, which means I went crazy and bought a day old pastry. Also note the exciting use of gold foil butter-wrappers. I'm a butter-my-bagel-guy.

I use only my hands for folding, ripping and twisting the napkins—no tools, no scissors, no glue except honey (especially if I'm sitting under a ceiling fan).

Most napkins have a grain. Rip with the grain and you get a nice straight line. Rip against the grain and you get a ragged edge. I chiefly use small square "bev naps," which have a more rigid structure, and dinner napkins, soft and sculptable—good for flowing drapes and rolling hills. If I really need structure, I turn to the bathroom. Trifold hand towels make a sharp fold and a sharp line. It's good to know your napkins.

Most of the pieces take thirty to ninety minutes to complete. The artwork is created on a table, photographed then removed and recycled. And sometimes I stuff the pieces in my pocket to reuse on another piece. I learned the hard way to double check pockets before laundering.

ABOUT QR CODES

This is a fun way to interact with *Playing with Napkins.* I was having coffee with my friend, Kevin Johnson, when he had the idea of linking my videos with QR Codes (Quick Response Codes). Several of the images in this book have "behind the scenes" videos that you can watch on a smart device (phone, tablet, etc.) with a QR code reader app. Perform an app search for "QR code reader" and you will find plenty of choices.

These video clips show part of the process or a technique, such as twisting, ripping, or folding. The clips vary in length, but the video for *Sunflowers* (page 95) shows the process from start to finish with commentary.

If you'd like to interact digitally with *Playing with Napkins,* you will need to download a QR code reader app for your smart device. Open the app and hold your device lens over the QR code. The app will link you to the video. Press play and enjoy.

If you'd like to watch the same videos on a computer or with a browser, you can visit PlayingWithNapkins.com and navigate to the videos page.

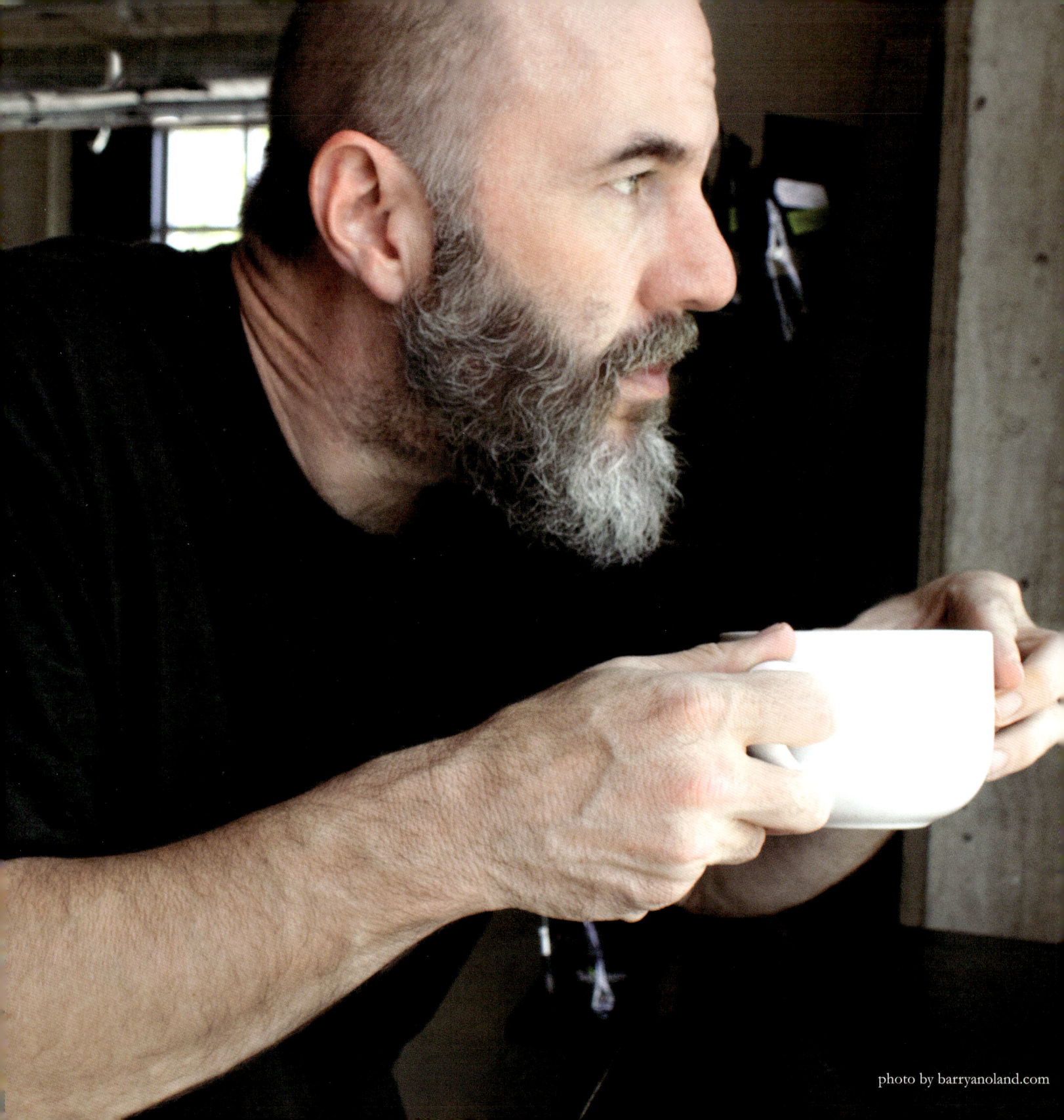

FOREWORD
by
Jeremy W. Childs

I first got to know Brian in the summer of 1988. At the time, he was living in my hometown of Colorado Springs, Colorado, and I was attending his old alma mater in Kankakee, Illinois. Sometimes we traveled back and forth together. You could say that our friendship was initially built on asphalt and black ice. There are few scarier drives than the one between Illinois and Colorado in the winter; and black ice is the most hideous devil I've had to deal with yet. Twenty-plus hours there, twenty-plus hours back. When you spend that kind of time with someone in a confined space, you know if they're going to be a pal or a foe.

But at first, Brian was neither. He was an enigma. I didn't know what to make of him. He was as free a spirit as I had ever met. Already prematurely balding, Brian let his hair grow long in the back so he could entertain people at parties with what he called "hair sculptures." He would use styling moose or hair gel or, frankly, whatever would do the trick and create abstract sculptures . . . on his head . . . with his hair.

I found his keen recall and detail on a vast array of subjects both fascinating and intimidating. How could one man know so much about everything? What part of the world produces the best goat cheese (and why), the best carpet to use in a high rise, the best way to build a mannequin, how to get tar off your car, the best herbal remedy for the shingles, how to change your brakes, or the best gas station to buy a hot dog, or . . . And all in explicit detail.

This was also a man who would often make his own clothes. In those days, he was pretty keen on purple. Instead of stitching with needle and thread, he used a hot glue gun. He has admitted to me on several occasions that he has done more than his fair of shopping at Lane Bryant, and wishes he had the guts to wear an Indian sarong in public. This is not Brian trying to be funny; it's just who he is. Understand that none of his clothing choices, even in the early years, had anything to do with what he found the most stylish (although color has always been important), but rather what was the most comfortable to wear. I've never met anyone who hates clothes as much as Brian Parker, and who wishes he could do without them altogether. If I've heard him say it once, I've heard him say it a thousand times, "If I were king of the world, life would be so easy. We would eat well, have our own personal chauffeurs, and not be required to wear clothes." Caution: It's good to call before you go over to his place.

Brian's passion has allowed me to see things I might have missed had I never met him. Over the years, he has taught me to see things with a new clarity. He likes what he likes and sees what he sees regardless of popularity or perceived reputation or taste. He is true to himself. For instance: He was blown away with the Salvador Dali Museum as well as the Andy Warhol exhibit at the Frist Center for Visual Arts in Nashville, but no more so than the cool and unusual cars at Nashville's Lane Motor Museum, or a certain brand of pig testicles. He was no more excited by one than the other. What fascinates, fascinates. What intrigues, intrigues.

An outstanding cook (yet another art form for him), the perfect meal may be Picholine olive-stuffed pork roast with cannellini beans or the combo meal at Burger King. This is the thing our twenty-six years of friendship is based upon. This the thing that won me over entirely. We all have our eccentricities. Brian just doesn't take himself so seriously as to let his get in the way of what is important. I have never known anyone more comfortable with who he is, and, thankfully, he is a bastion of humility with a seemingly endless reservoir of talent. You just couldn't ask for a better pal.

I've witnessed firsthand Brian's processes and creations in computer graphics, acrylic, plaster, foam core, wood, sand, cardboard, papier-mâché, fabric, chicken wire, flowers, spaghetti (finding the right pasta length is more difficult than you might think), and in about a dozen other media I can't recall at this moment, and that I'm relatively sure the art community doesn't recognize yet. Case in point: napkins.

Give the man a roll of gaff tape, a sweet pickle and a few packing peanuts and I swear he will somehow, almost mystically, provide your heart's desire. A portrait? No problem. Perhaps a still life of *Allegory of Sunset Air* or a miniature of the Taj Mahal or the Hagia Sophia? Why not? Simply put, Brian is a brilliant, sensitive, hilarious, wise, beautiful, zenned-out freak of nature. And in typical Parker fashion, this book is his love letter to the art that made him that way.

Brian must create. It is not a sense of legacy that seems to drive the man, but rather the desire to make something beautiful out of the moment he is in. As is often the case with him, when any given moment is over, so is the art he may have temporarily created. Thankfully, in Brian Parker universe, there are exceptions to his usual sensibilities. There are a few moments here and there worth living again before they are tossed in the trash can with half eaten muffins and old coffee grounds. Thankfully, he said: "I think I'll take a photo of what I did with these napkins before I toss them away."

I connect with this book, with this strange experiment, because to me it says: "You can find the Mona Lisa anywhere." You may have to roll up your sleeves and hunt for her. She may be staring up at you from the garbage with moldy eyes waiting for you to reinvent her, but she is there--in some moment, somewhere. She is saying, "Don't forget to play, don't forget to find me." I think maybe it's for people who think weird like that. Or maybe it's for people who just think it's crazy that he can do this with napkins. Or maybe it's for people who like to spend a cool Sunday morning at the coffee shop wishing they had something more productive to do with their time than sit at a coffee shop on a cool Sunday morning. But probably, it's for all of us.

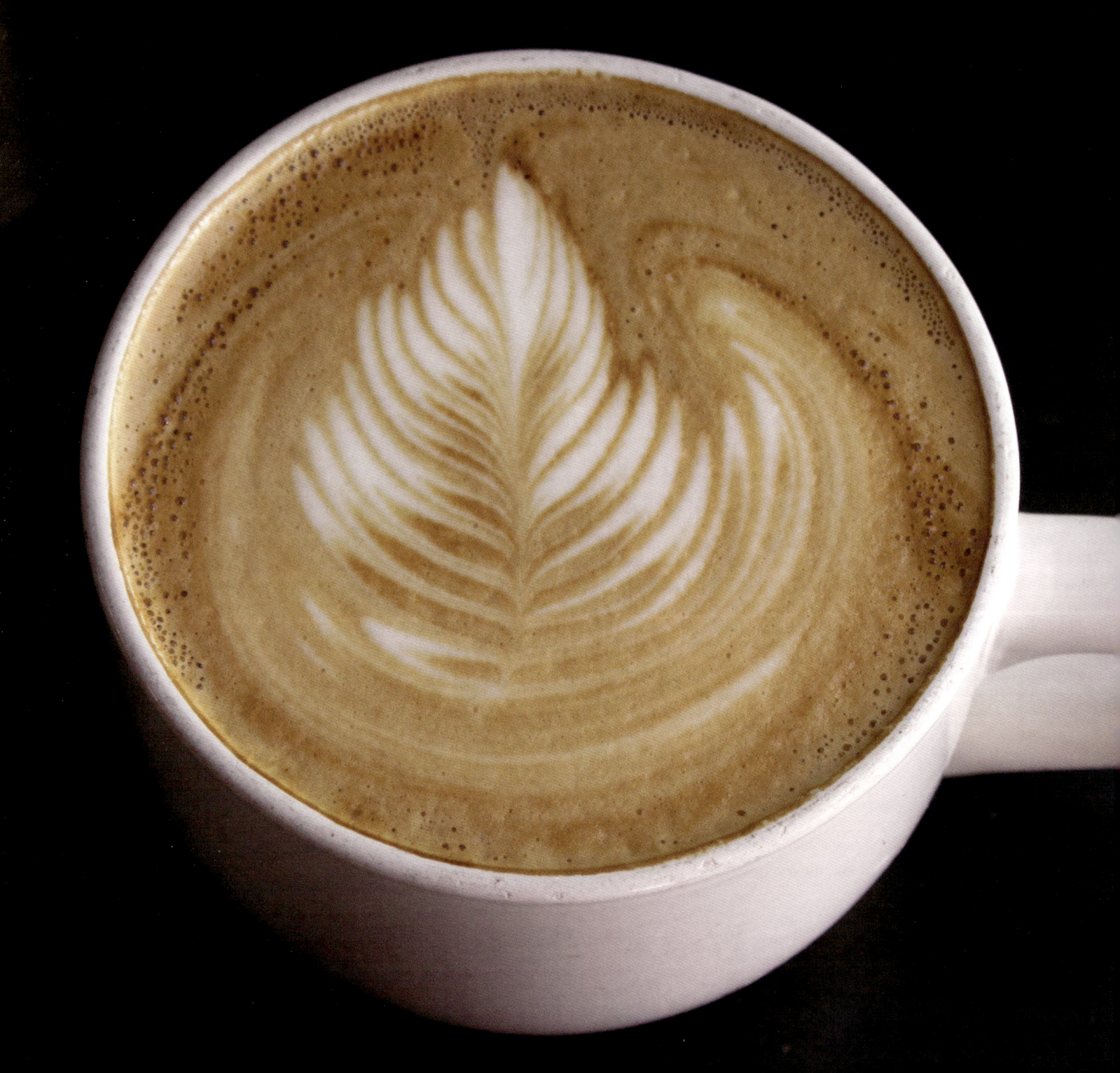

PREFACE

It all started with fidgety fingers at my local coffee house.

Retract that. Back up. It all started with my fidgety fingers at church. I was a restless kid. Mom would give me Doublemint gum to curb my energy during sermons. It was a double treat for me because I discovered an art medium in the gum wrappers. I would create fans and birds and things—all from the Wrigley's green paper and foil wrappers. My favorite thing in the world was to make art from nothing.

I came by it honestly. We were a family of artists and had every conventional art medium at our disposal. But I most often chose paper. Old newspapers and giant rolls of raw newsprint, crepe paper, wrapping paper, tissue paper, scroll paper, typing paper, and old magazines all found their way into my busy hands. I learned how to make origami frogs and ducks, paper airplanes and helicopters and boats, telescoping ladders and palm trees, papier-mâché, sculptures, entire bouquets of crepe paper flowers, and intricate floral scroll work on family photos and documents. It didn't feel like an obsession. But, as this book proves, it was.

Like many other great things in life, this collection of artwork happened by surprise. My husband Barry and I have a Sunday morning routine of coffee and a bagel at Ugly Mugs.

One particular day, I was fiddling with my napkin and spoon and made an angel from the trash on the table. It wasn't intentional. I was just playing, sort of daydreaming with my fingers. The angel just sort of appeared. I shared the pic online, and people liked it. So I kept creating pieces and playing with napkins became a "thing." Then a year or so later, with many encouragements, it became this book.

I have been an artist and designer for nearly thirty years. I have received much applause and numerous awards for my professional work. I've judged several national and local Emmy competitions, and won a few myself. My commercial portfolio is impressive, but nothing has ever captured an audience like my humble, throw-away napkin art. It is a curious thing.

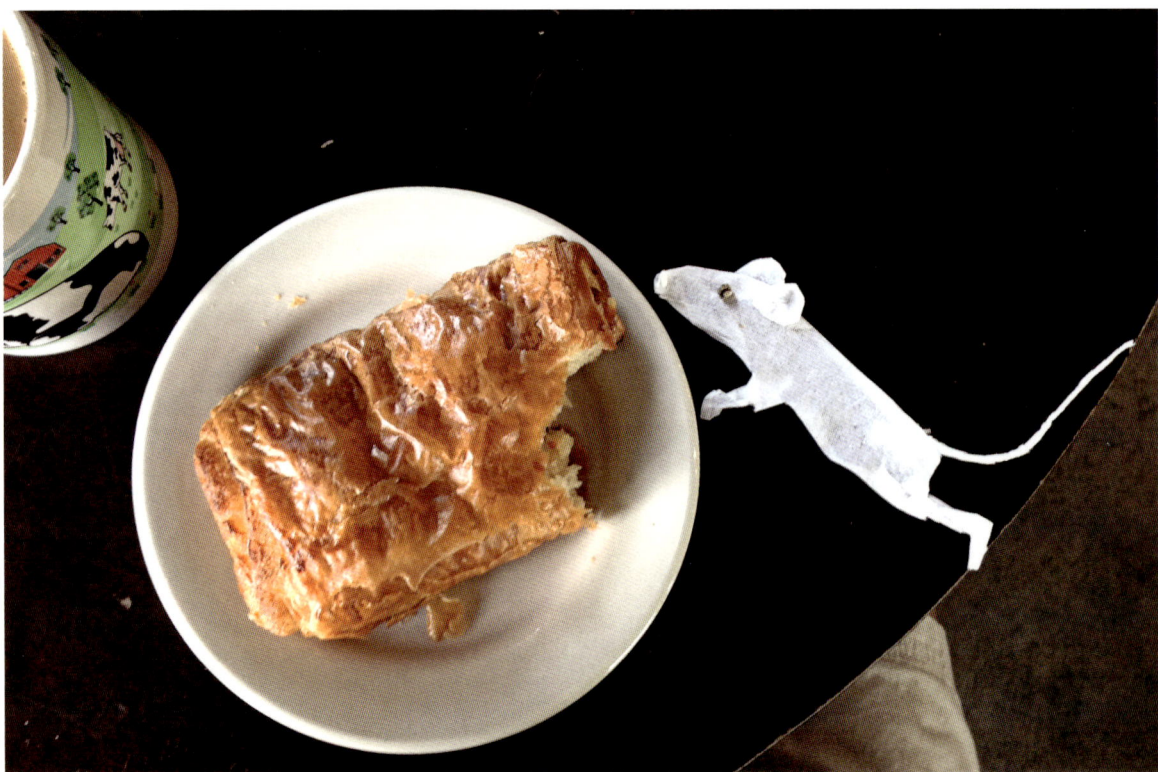

INTRODUCTION

I didn't realize it at first, but *Playing with Napkins* is largely autobiographical. When I started planning the book, I decided to add certain subjects that would attract certain demographics. I made a list and weighed the gravity of each audience. I wanted "this" audience and "that" audience. I wanted them all.

But in the end, I decided against strategizing. I stopped questioning and followed my instincts. I was pleased that the resultant body of artwork reflected my life. With few exceptions, the images depict masterpieces I have seen in person, places I've visited, or things I've seen or love.

Playing with Napkins is an art book, but it also celebrates the joy and random beauty of play. It's an easily forgotten habit. But play is good for you. A sense of play helps you see things in a different way. Play prompts the best question in the world, "What if?" Ask yourself "What if I did this? What if this happened?" and maybe you reply "Oh! That would be funny or shocking or new—maybe a new path!" Play helps train your mind to examine possibilities. And possibilities are endless.

Play also improves physical heatlth, mental health, and relationships. Search the internet for the "power of play," and you will have volumes to read on the subject. It is an important, powerful skill that we too often abandon with adulthood. I am not referring to playing a game or watching TV or looking at a device. The type of play that I am talking about should not require equipment. It should not have rules. It is aimless, untethered occupation with your mind and your environment.

What if the path to a better life was the path of play? What if doing what comes naturally and doing what is fun was good for you? What if it was also good for the people you love? Well, it is.

I hope you enjoy the art in this book, but my best hope is that you will be inspired to play more. We could all use more play in our lives. Look at a napkin, your keys, your life, and ask yourself, "What if?" Maybe we could all discover something new.

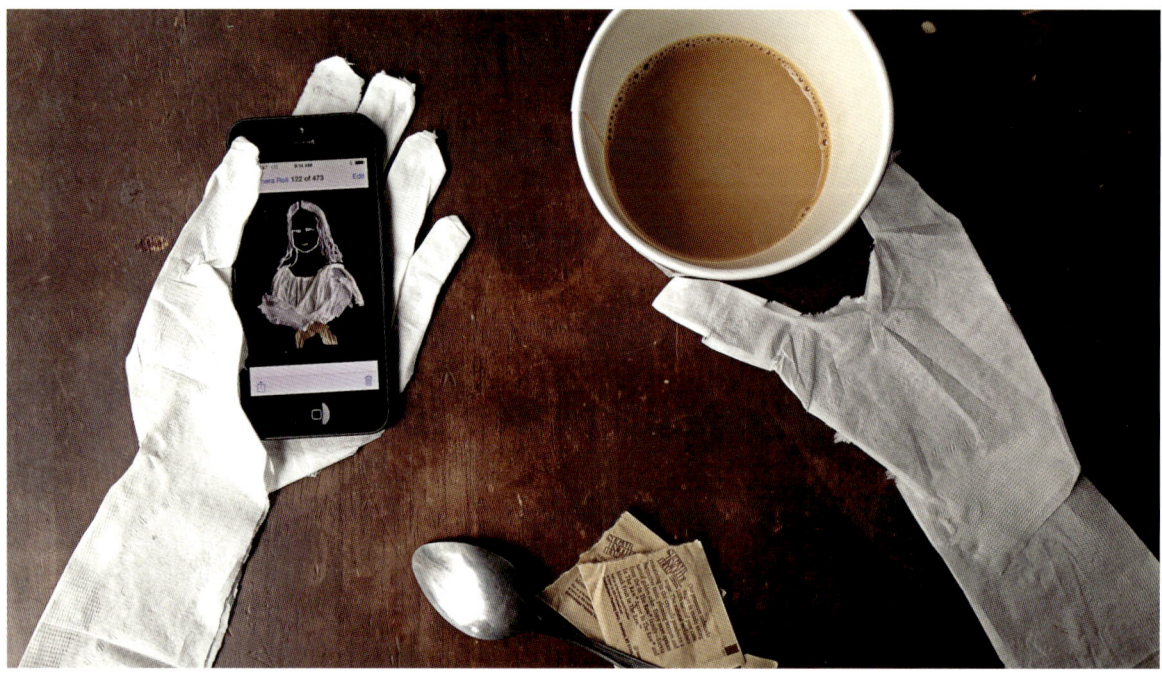

THE MASTERS

Recreations of the Great Masterpieces

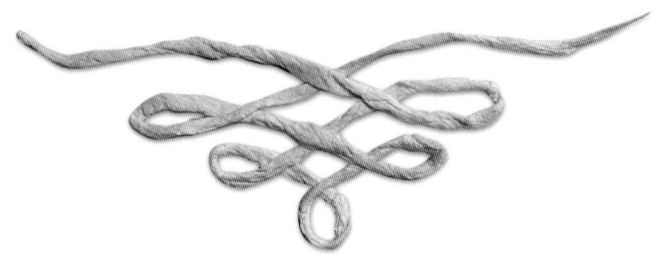

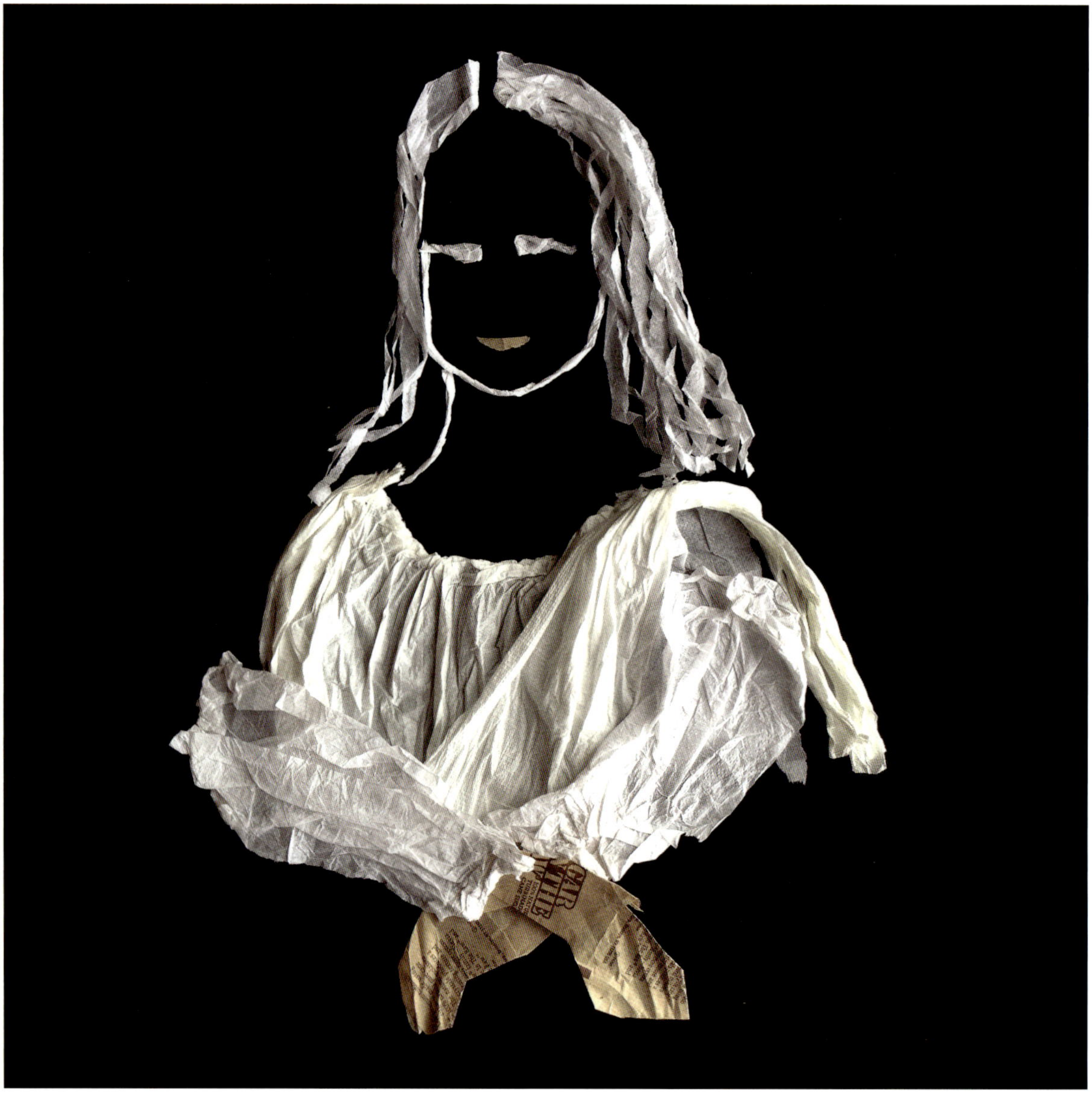

Mona Lisa
Leonardo daVinci, 1505

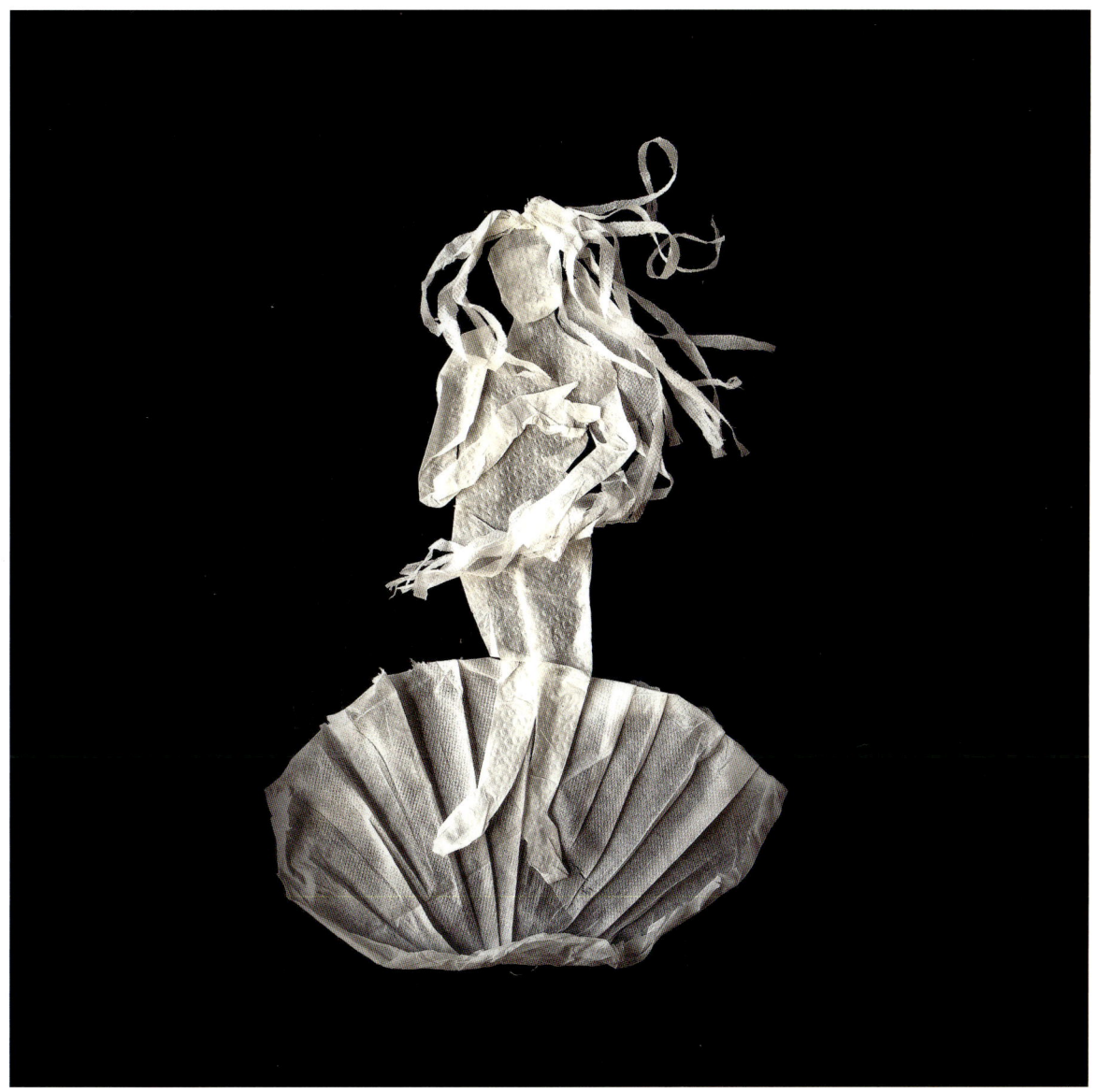

Birth of Venus
Sandro Boticelli, 1486

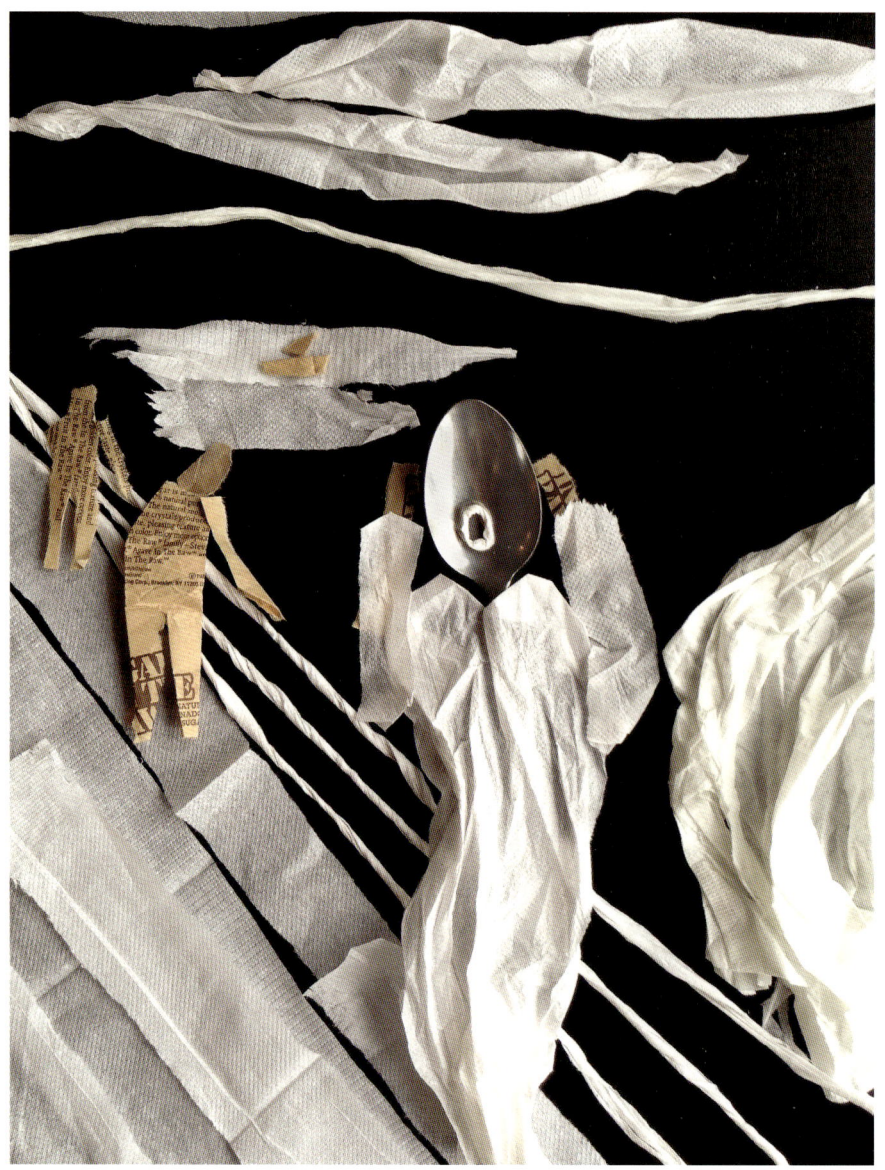

The Scream
Edvard Munch, 1893

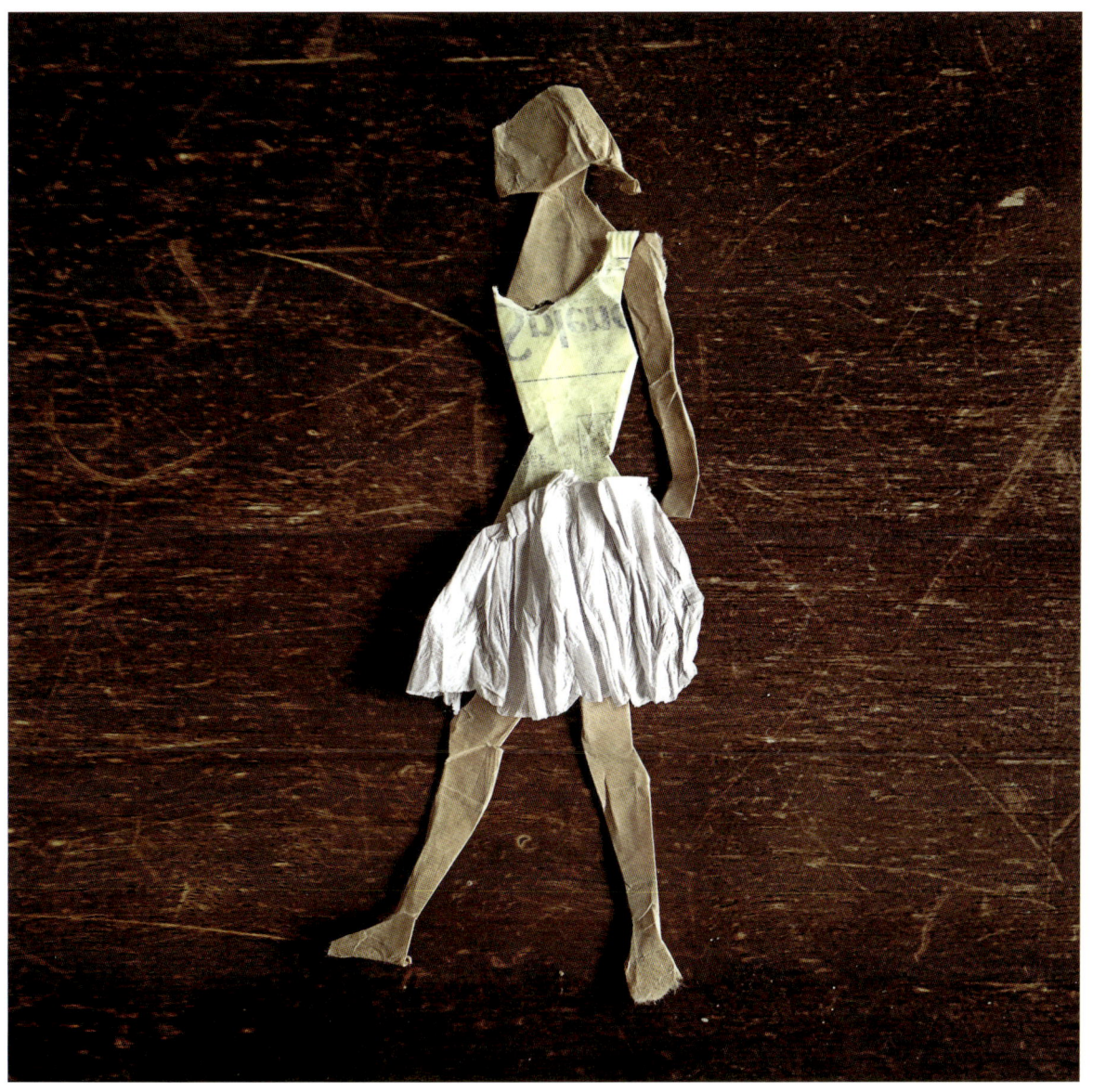

Little Fourteen-Year-Old Dancer
Edgar Degas, 1878

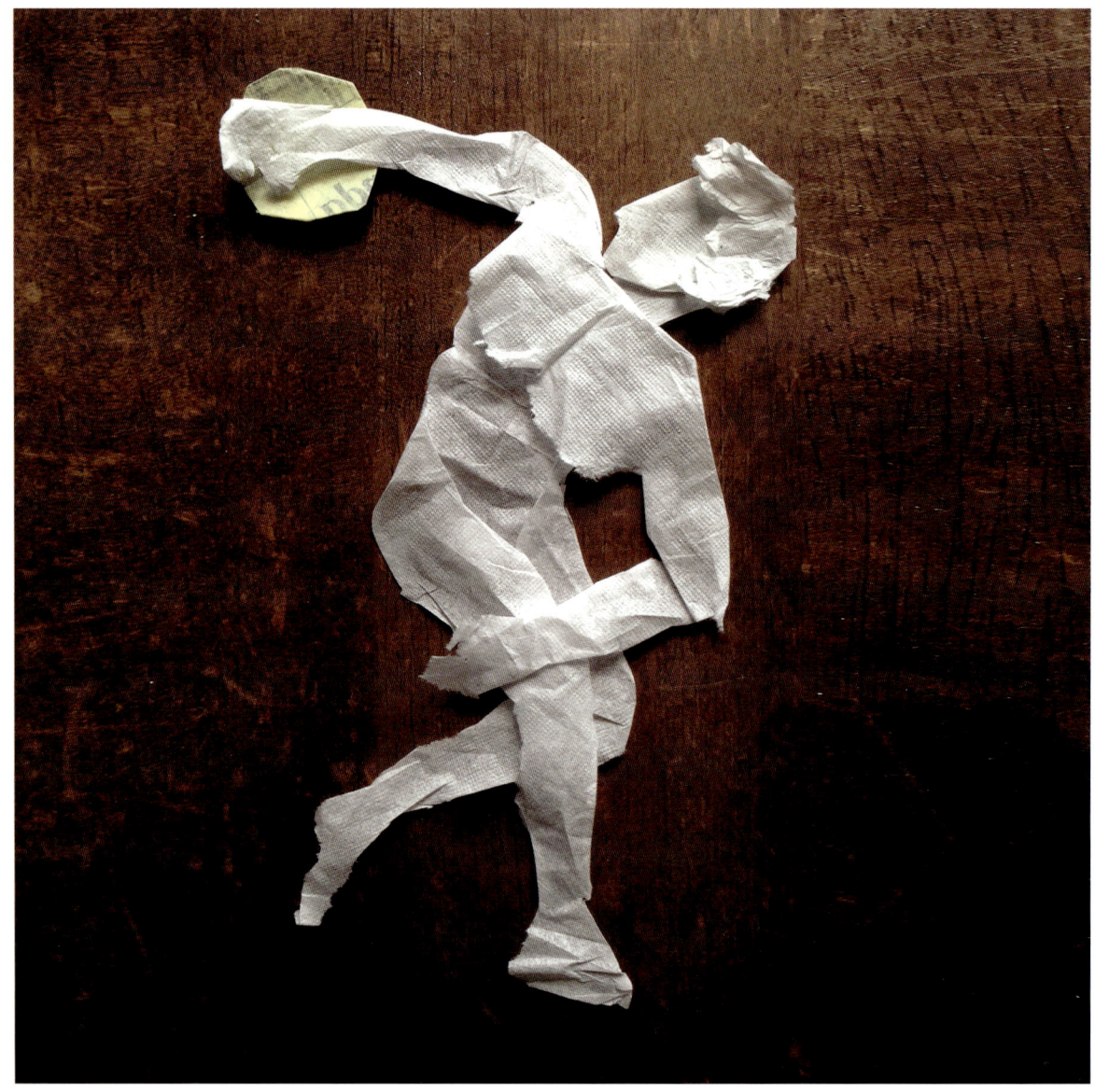

Discobolus
Myron, circa 460-450 bce

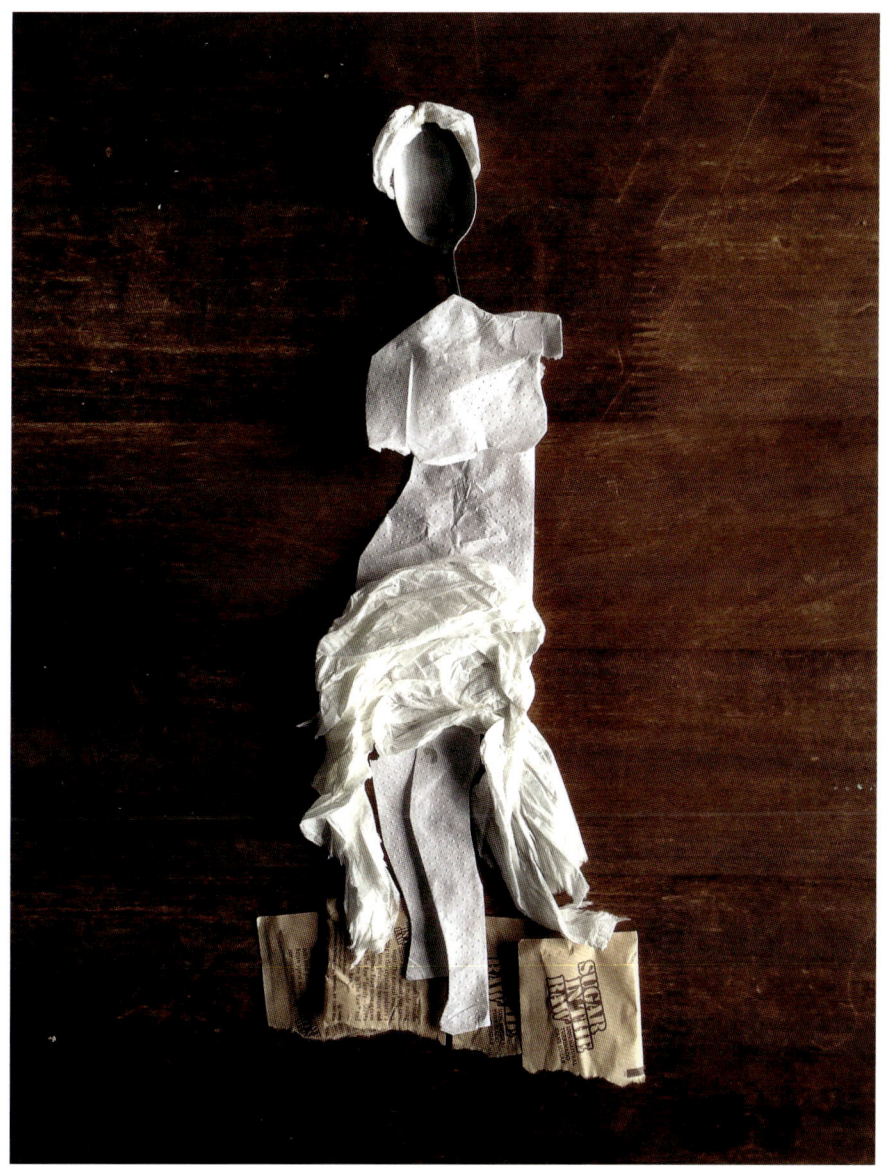

Venus de Milo
Alexandros of Antioch, 115 bce

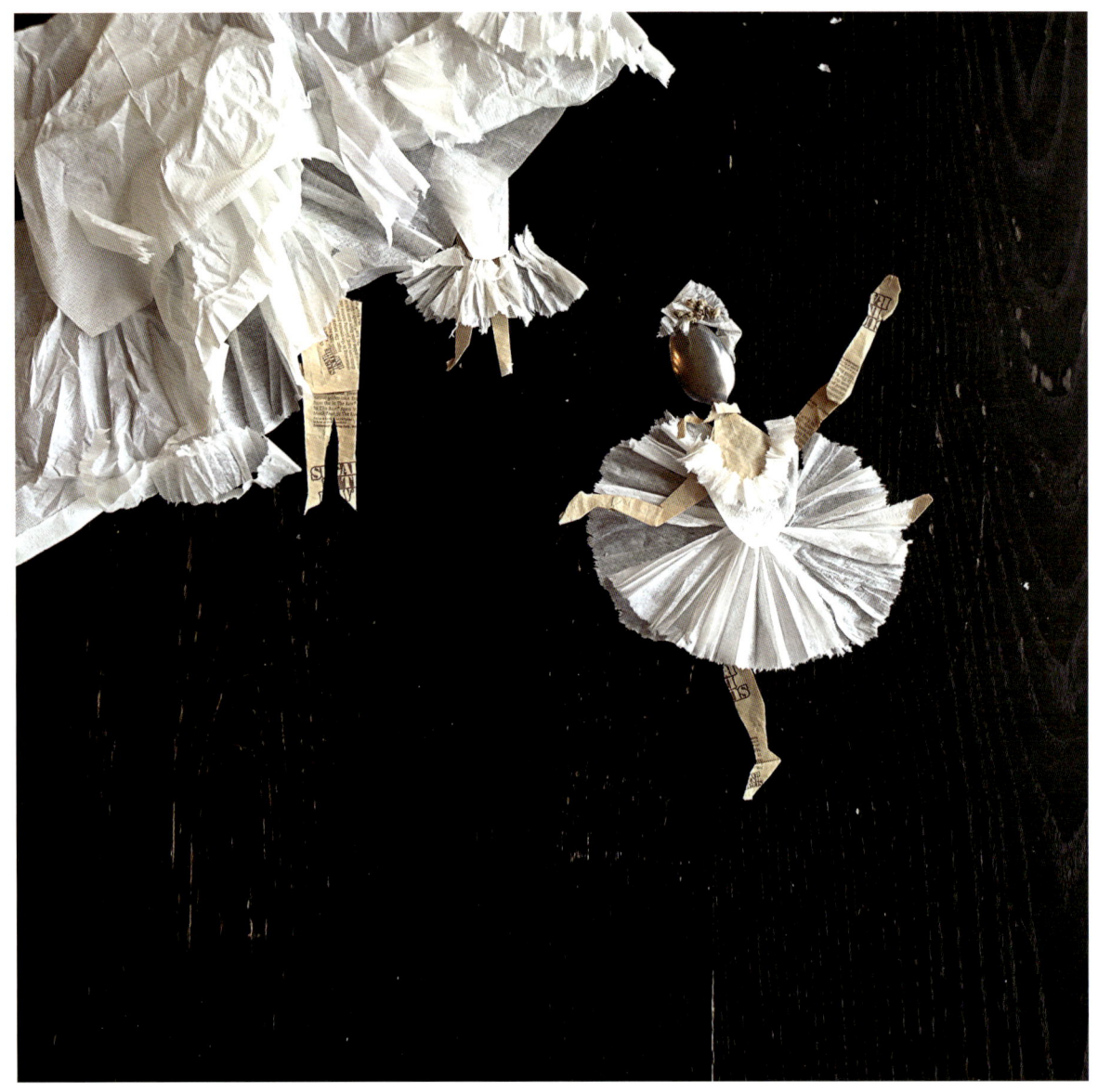

L'etoile
Edgar Degas, 1878

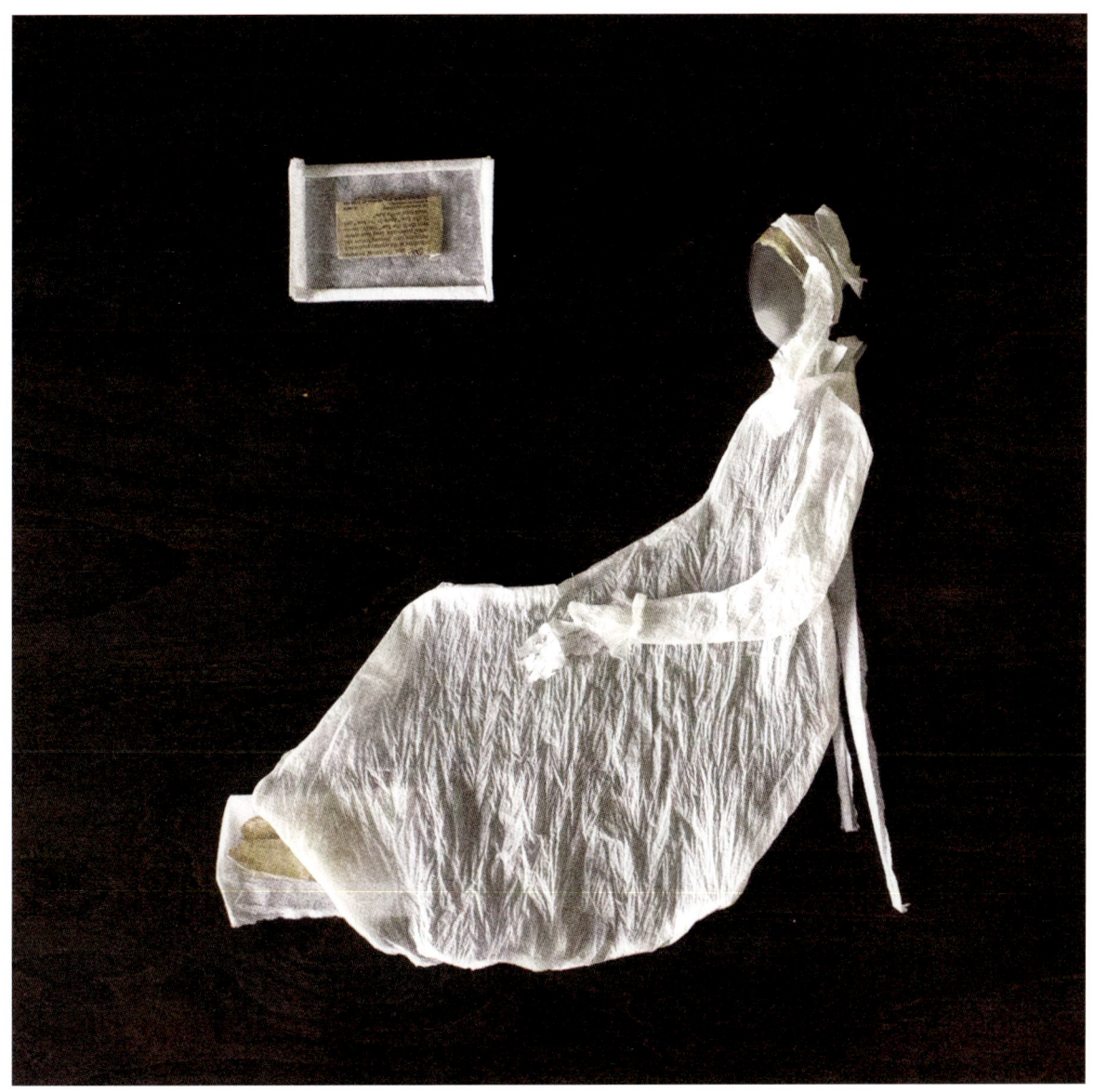

Whistler's Mother
James McNiell Whistler, 1871

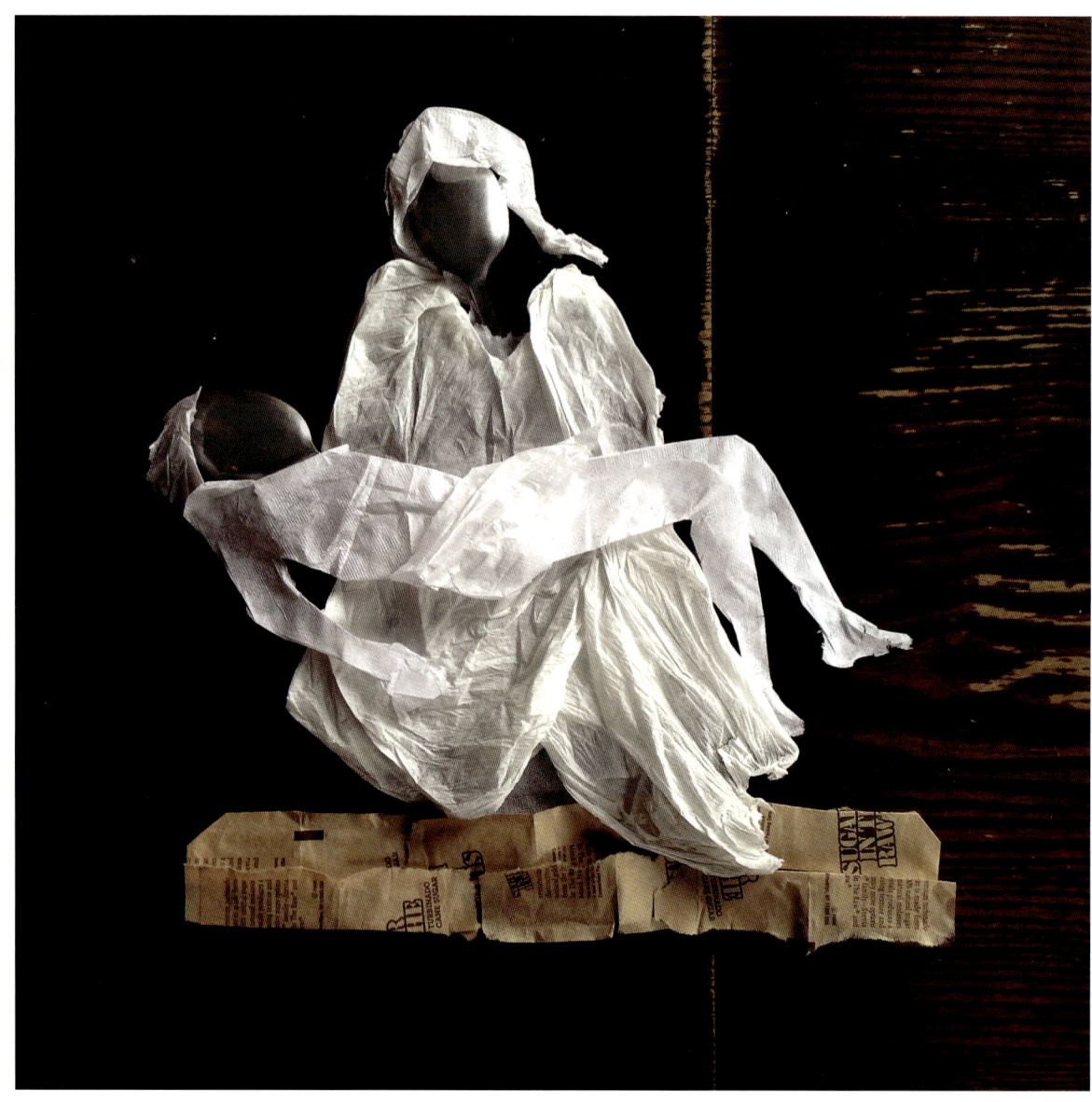

The Pieta
Michelangelo, 1498-1499

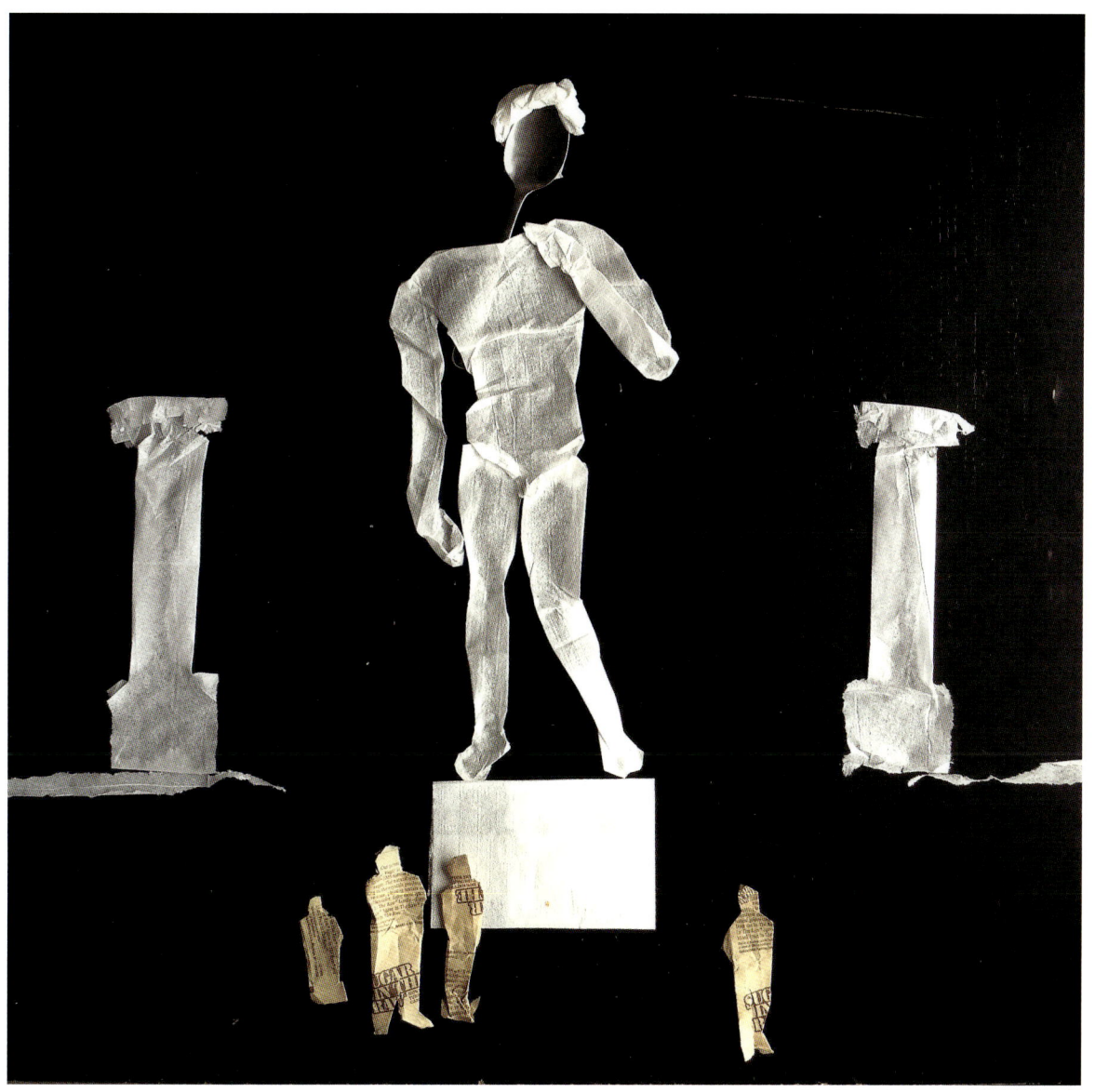

The David
Michelangelo, 1504

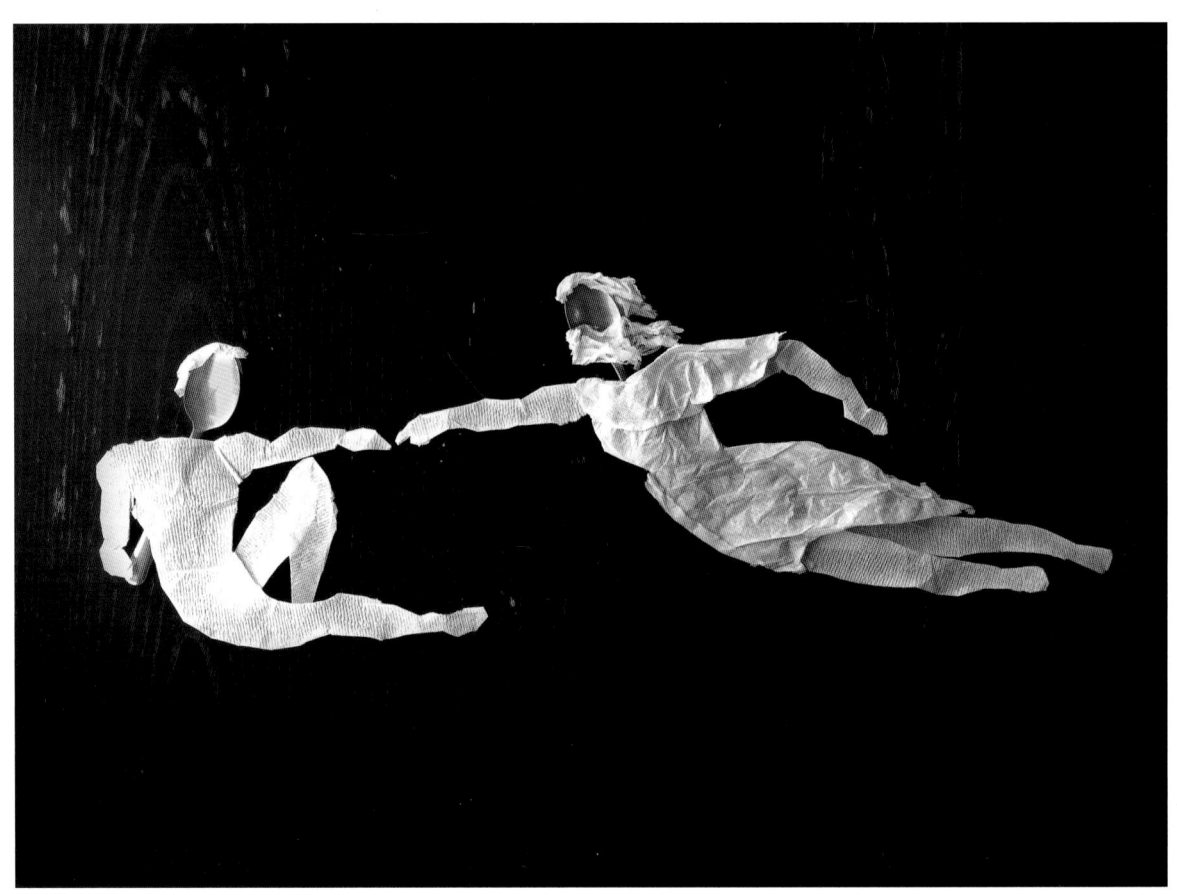

The Creation of Adam, Sistine Chapel
Michelangelo, 1512

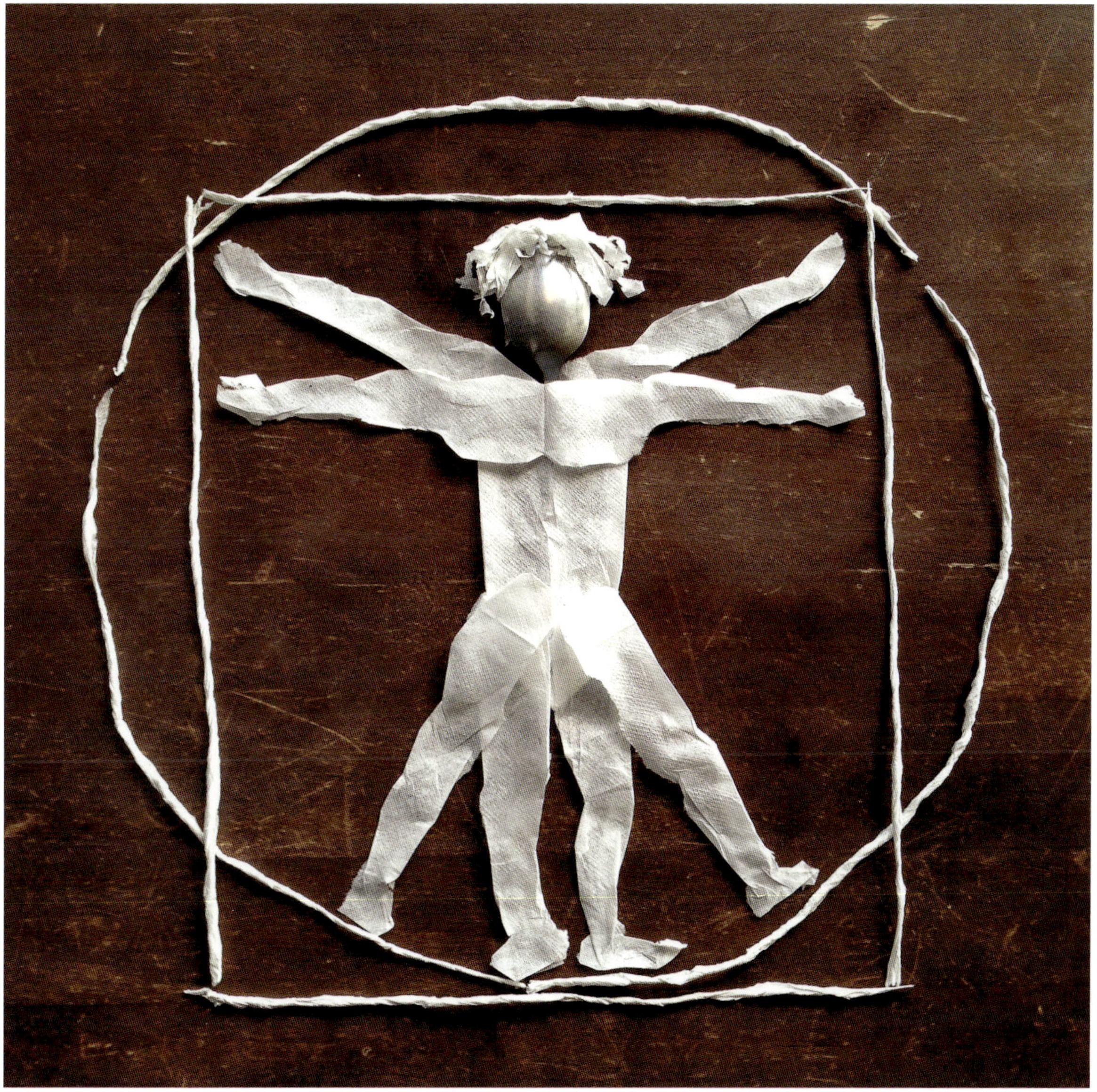

Vitruvian Man
Leonardo daVinci, 1490

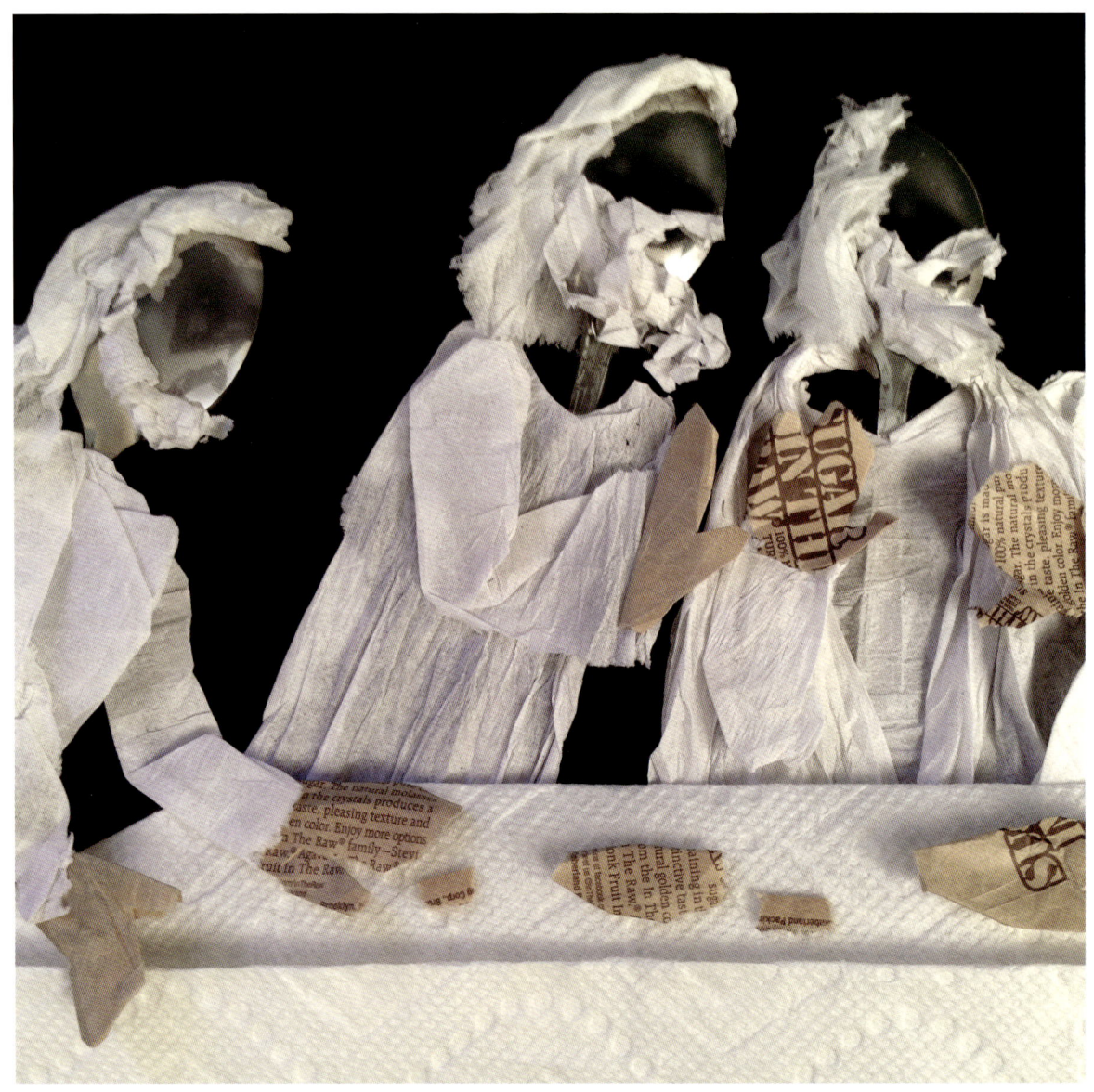

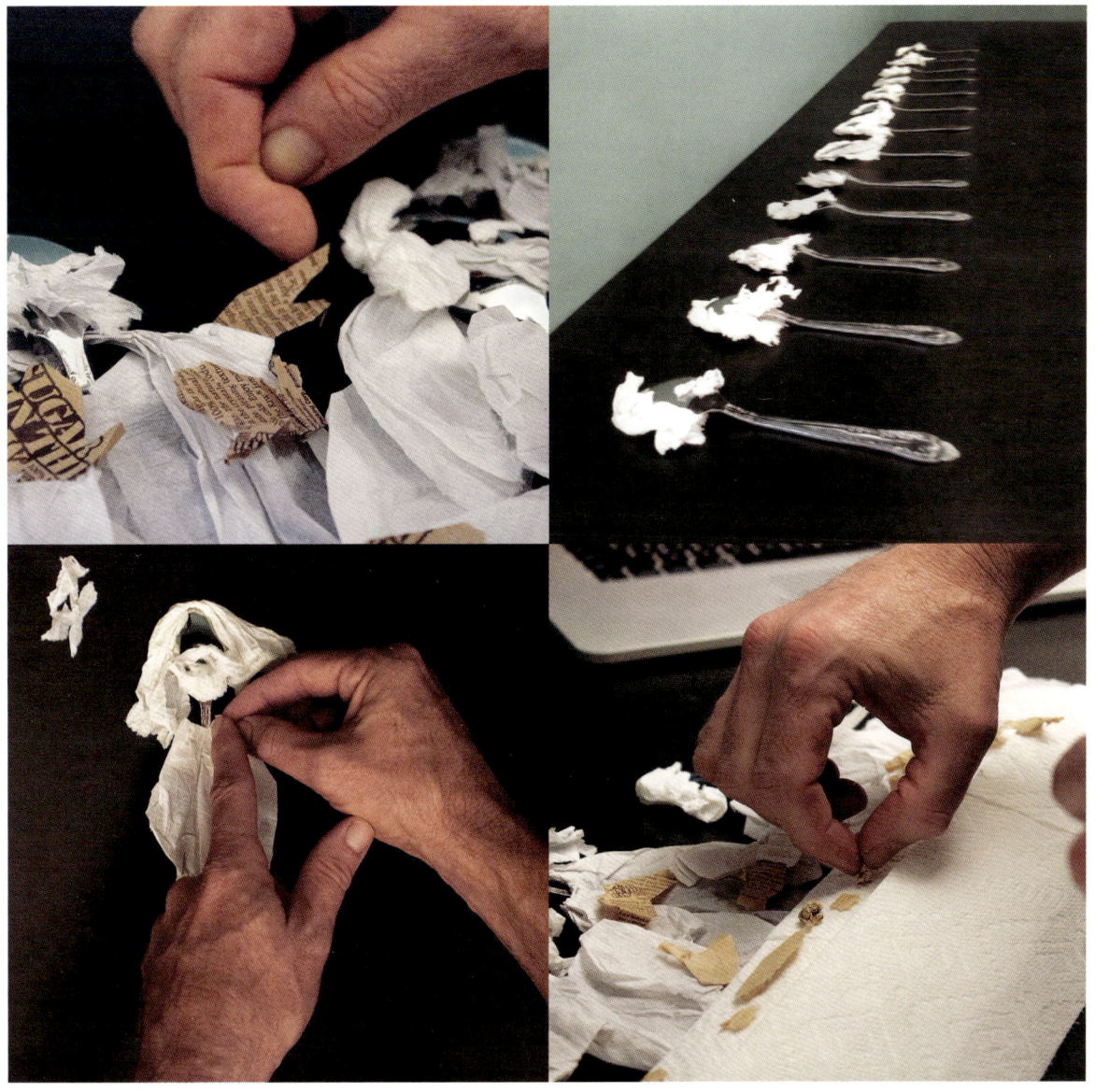

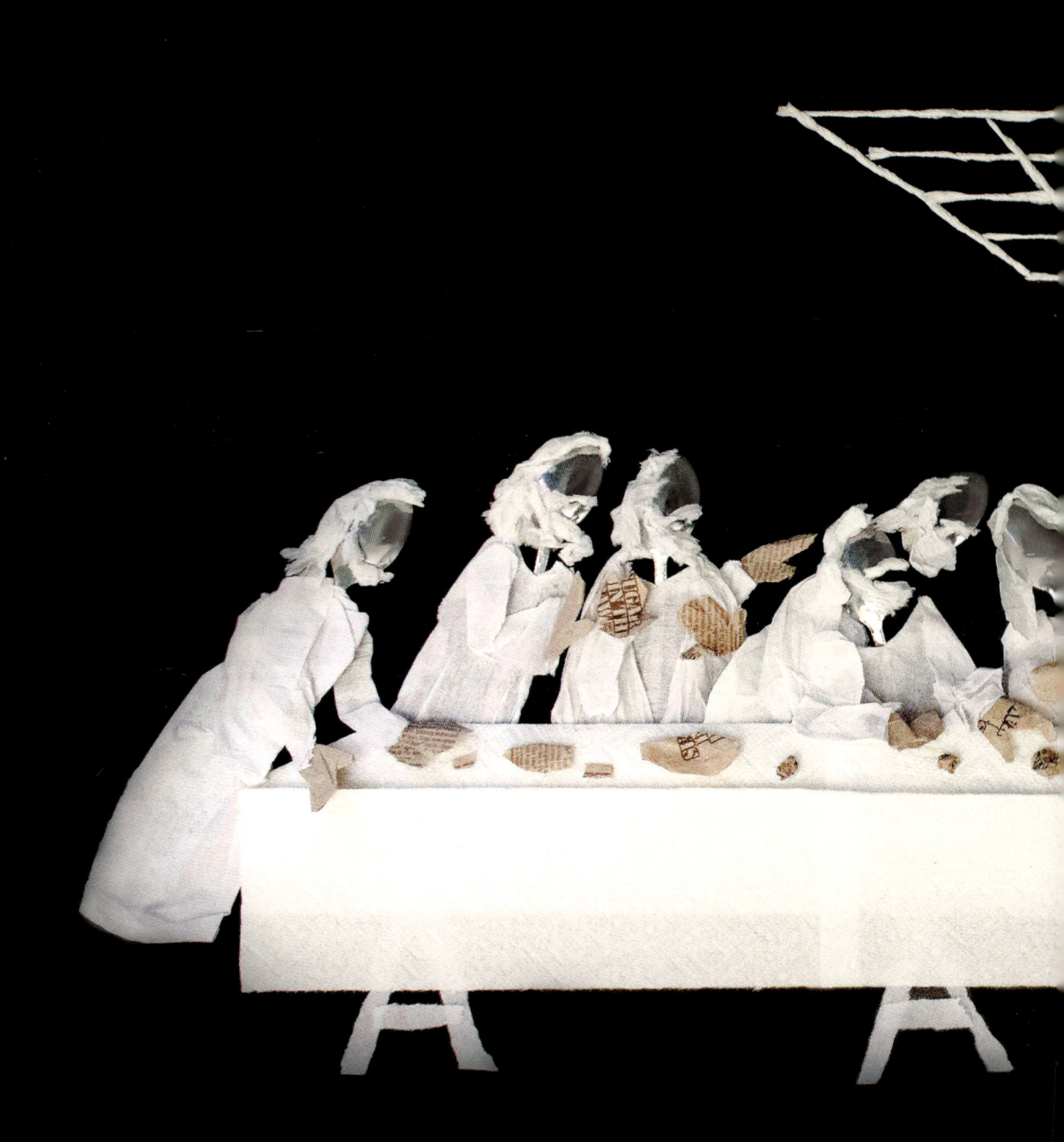

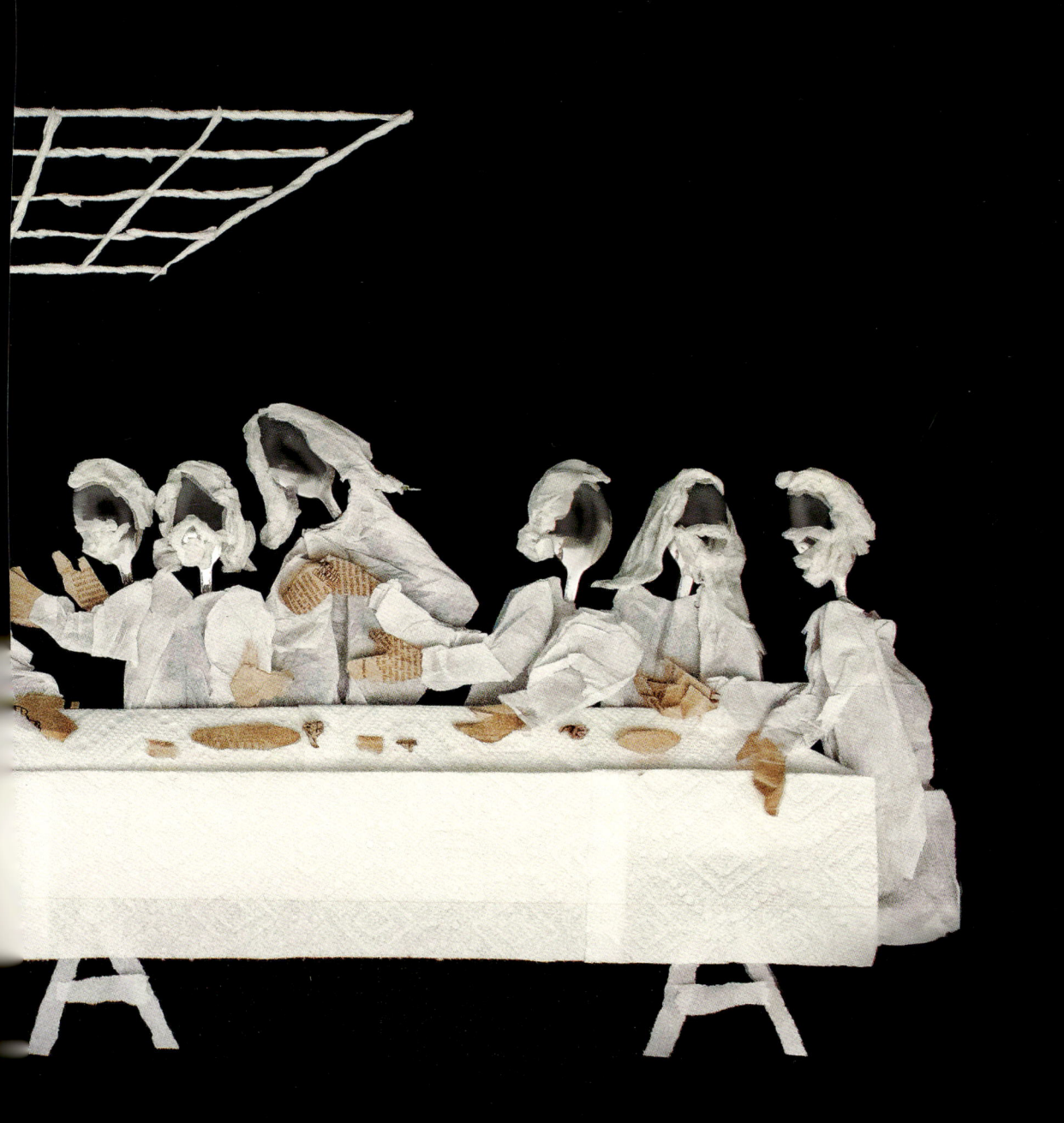

THE LAST SUPPER

I thought about recreating *The Last Supper* in napkins several times, but I was daunted by the amount of time and detail it would require. Barry would be sipping coffee for hours. It was crazy. I dismissed the idea and kept to hour-long creations on our Sunday morning trips to the coffee shop.

But *The Last Supper* nagged at me. I decided that our kitchen counter would be my canvas. It would provide a nice black background and it was open 24/7. I started on a Saturday, hoping to finish by Sunday morning. After an hour, I realized I wasn't getting what I wanted. I changed direction and decided to use thirteen spoons for the figures. I liked the scale. Re-inspired, I literally tore into the project. Time was disappearing and sleep was looming. I reached a comfortable point and stopped for the night.

I went to bed with a good, tired sigh. My back hurt from bending over the counter, my whole body intent on such minute work. I stretched a little and smiled, feeling happy with the way it was coming together.

I woke early, still tasked with a few robes and the table. After an hour, the figures were done, but I didn't like the softness of the table. I switched to paper towel and it worked. It provided structure and contrast to the billowy clothes. I finished and shared it online Sunday morning. It required more time and fewer napkins than I would have guessed:

The Last Supper required:
Nine and one-half hours to complete
Thirteen spoons
Two paper towels
Four napkins
Four sugar packets

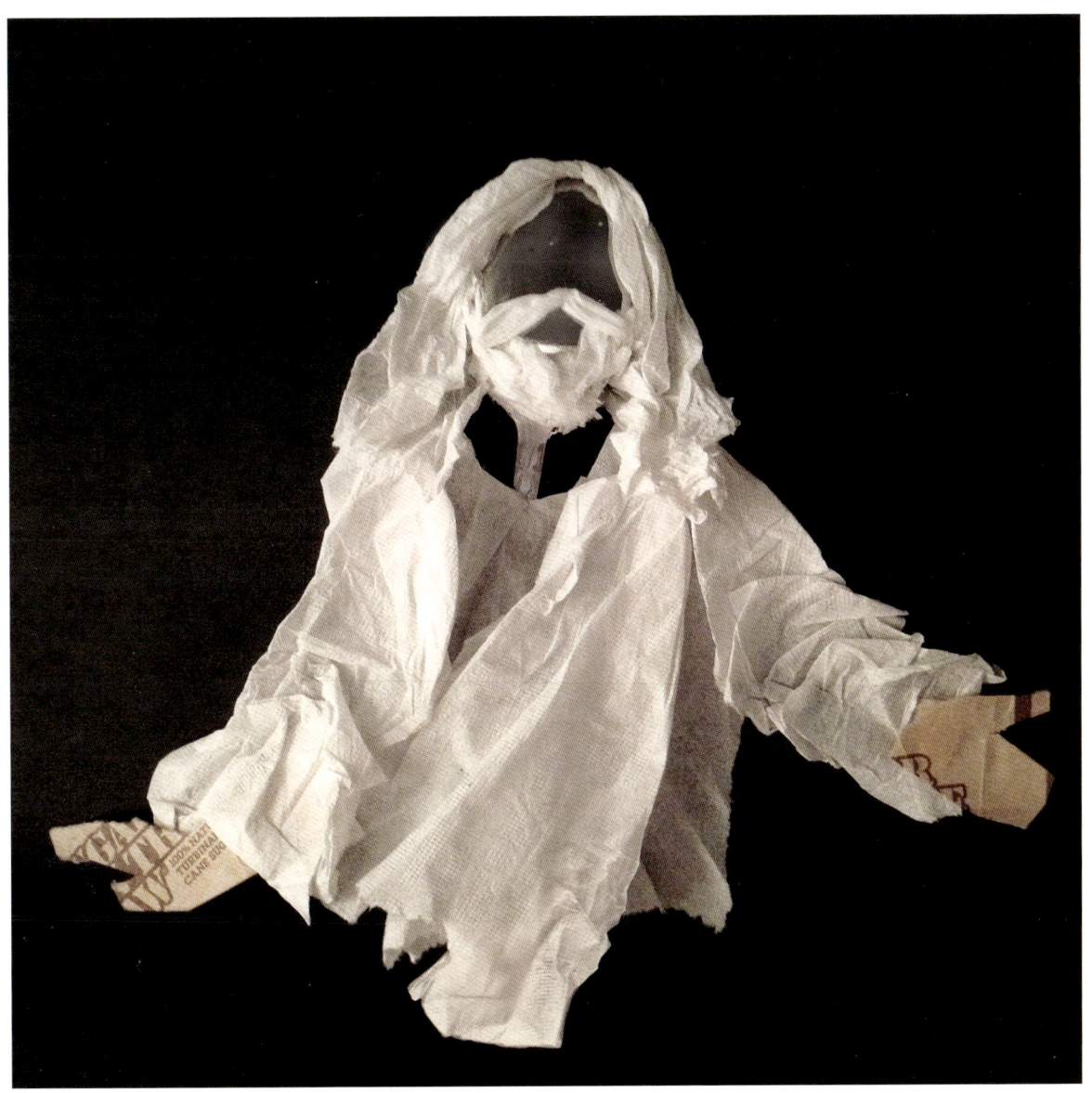

Jesus from *The Last Supper*

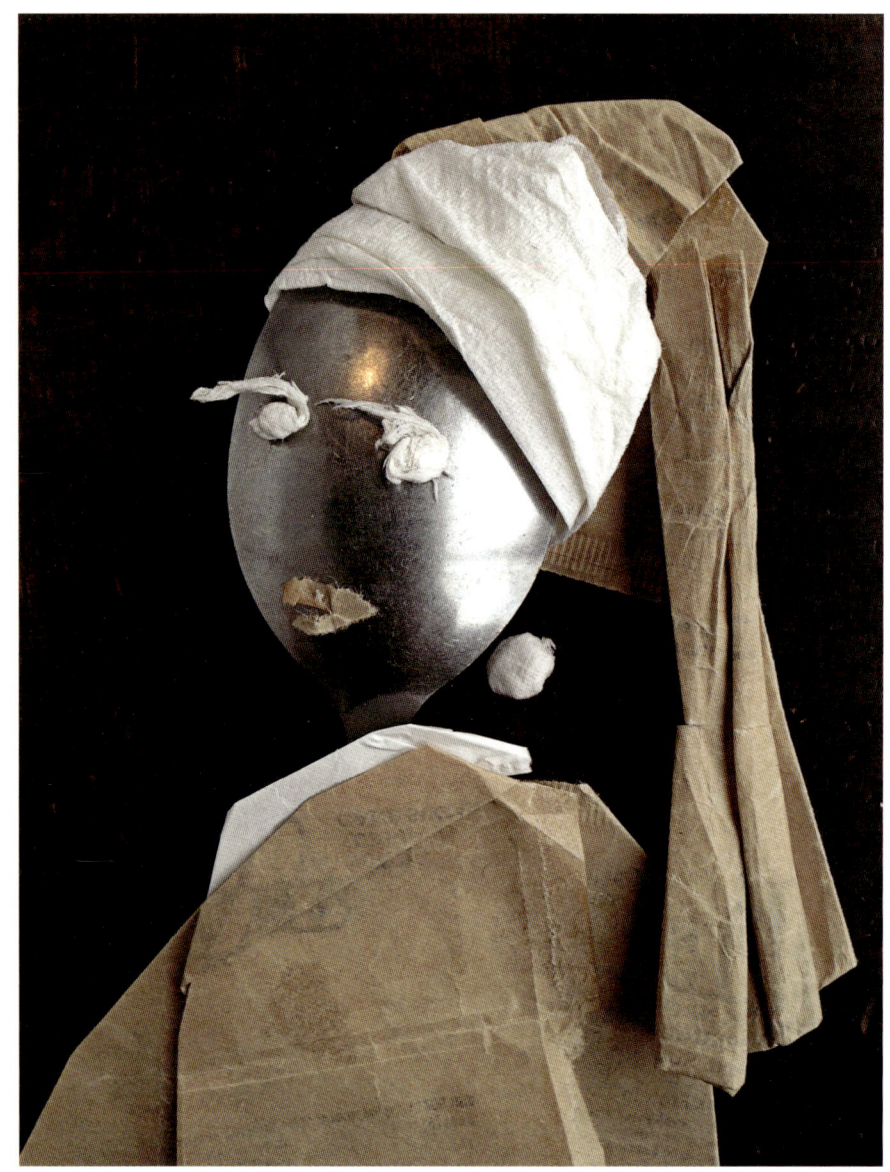

Girl with the Pearl Earring
Johannes Vermeer, 1665

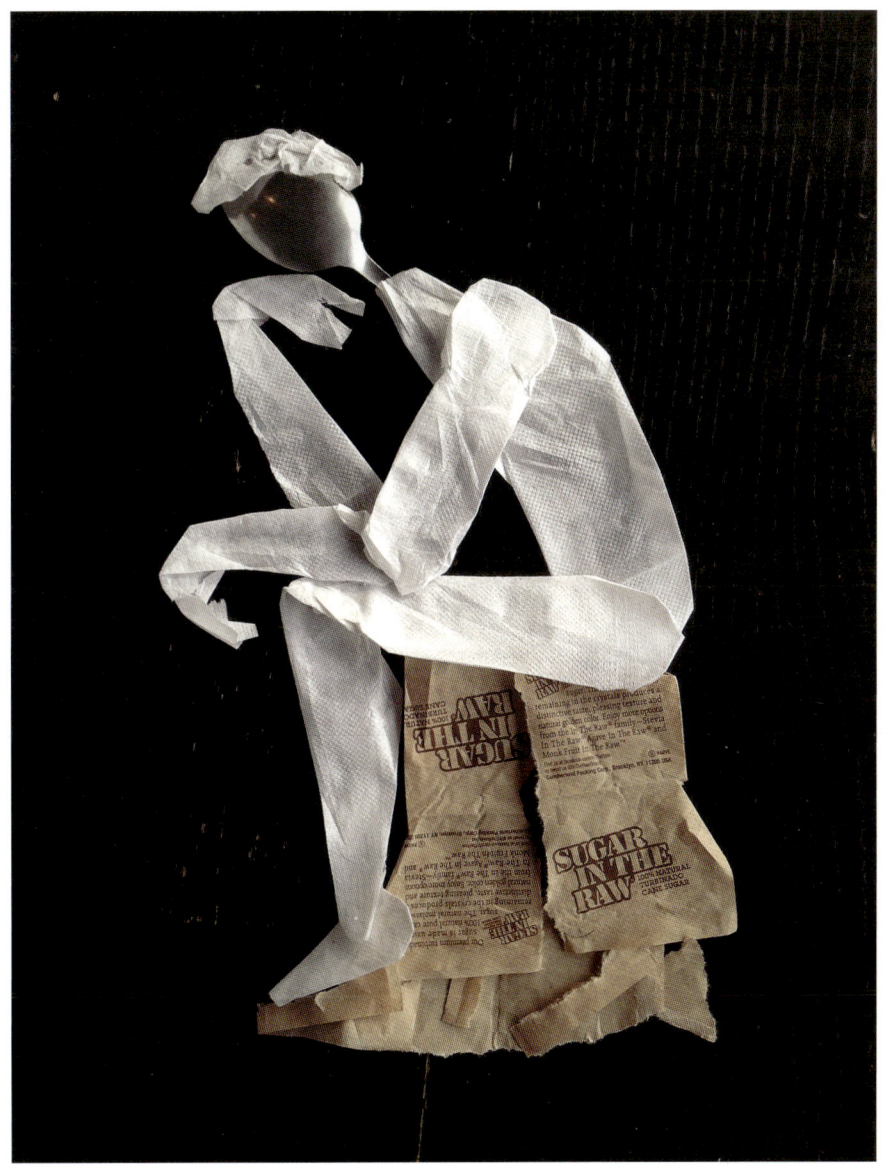

The Thinker
Auguste Rodin, 1905

TWO SISTERS

When I was growing up, even our board games leaned toward the arts. I loved the art auction game, Masterpiece. I admired the wealthy bidders in the box top photo and the masterpieces themselves. There were two specific game cards I treasured above all others: the reproduction of Renoir's Two Sisters, and the persona card for Roxy "Big D" Warrenson.

At the beginning of the game each player assumes the persona of a particular art collector. My brother Jim's favorite persona was Count Francois Du Bonnet. With chestnut hair and tailored suit, he was a dashing 007 type. With equal flair, my Roxy sported a platinum blonde perm and pearls the size of jawbreakers. She seemed like a gal who was up for some Doublemint gum and a good time. Roxy was a flashy, glamorous art collector and I wanted to be her. Every single time.

The *Two Sisters* card was the most exciting, most romantic image I had ever seen. Those luminescent, beflowered young girls cast a spell on me. My heart just went out to them. The reds were so vibrant against the soft floral hues. I didn't care about strategy or winning; I just wanted that bewitching piece of art at any cost. When that painting came up for auction, I threw caution to the wind and outbid everyone. Every single time.

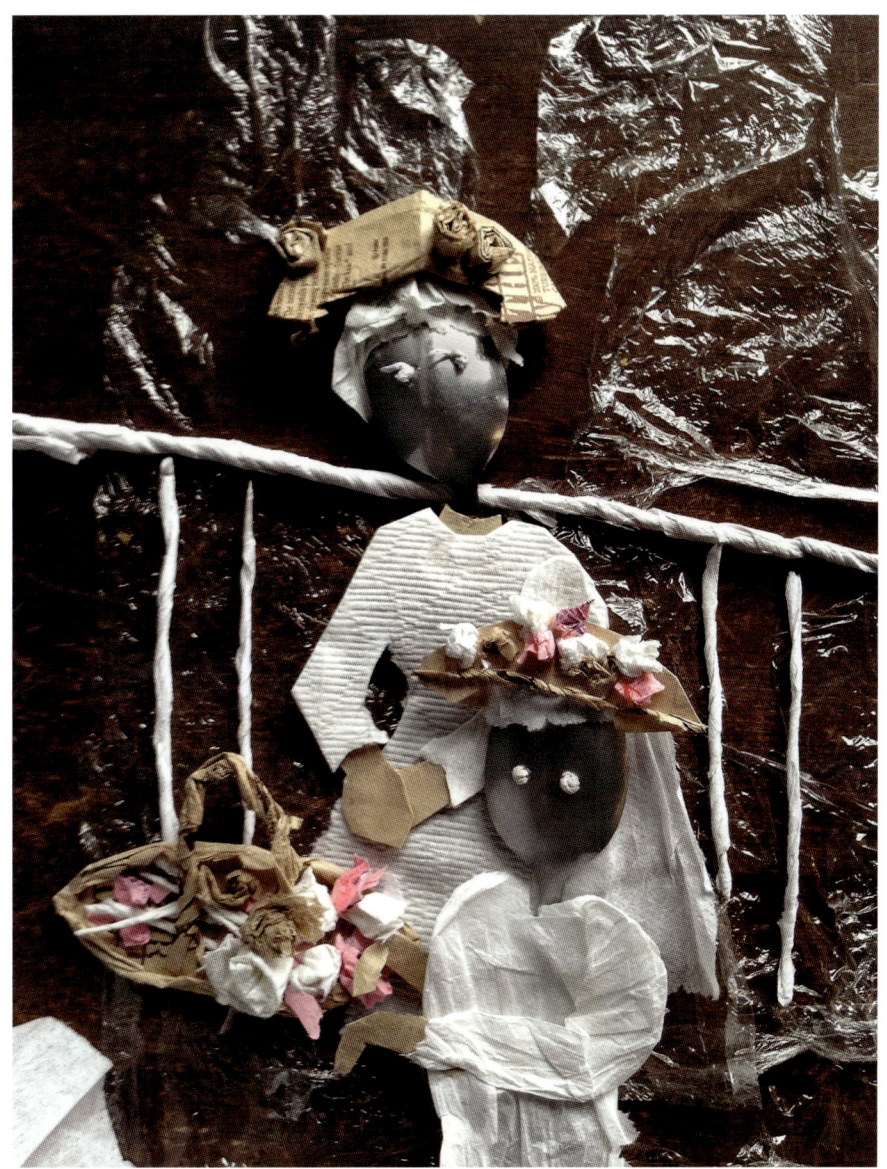

Two Sisters
Pierre-Auguste Renoir, 1881

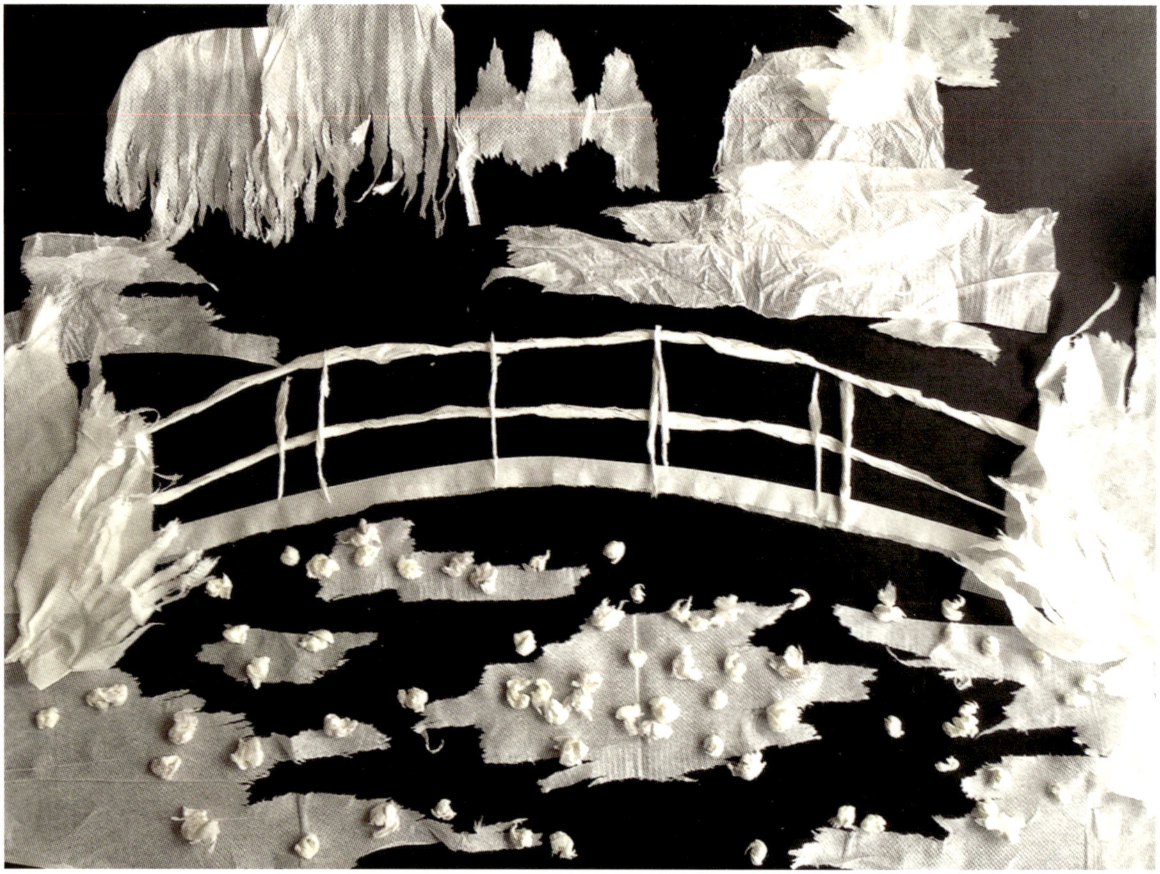

Water Lillies at Giverny Pond
Claude Monet, 1919

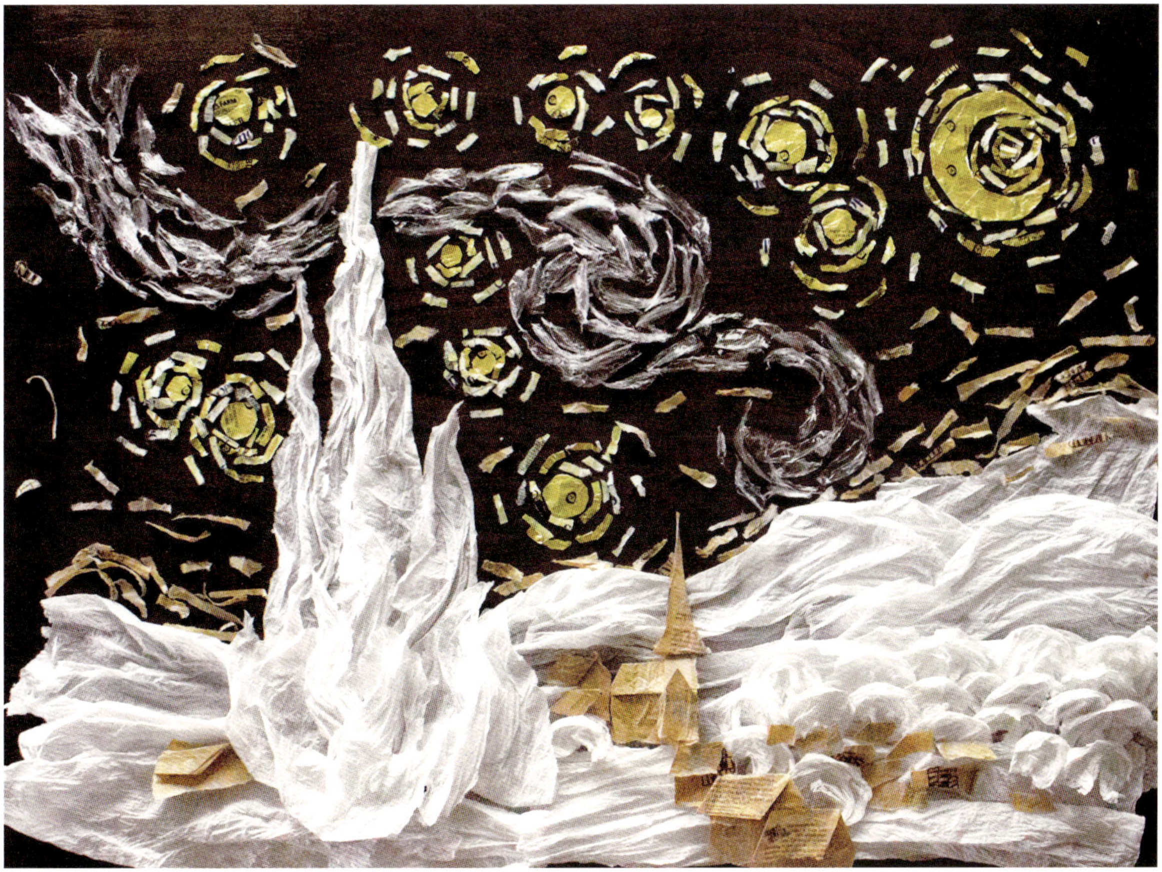

The Starry Night
Vincent van Gogh, 1889

THE WORLD

A Survey of Travel & Leisure

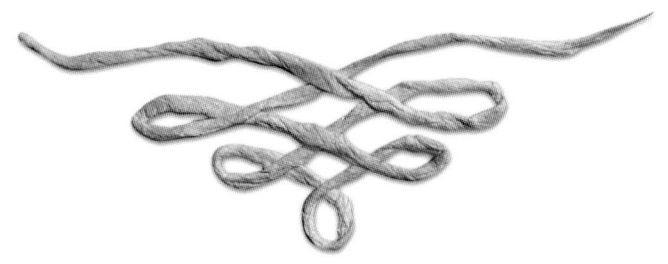

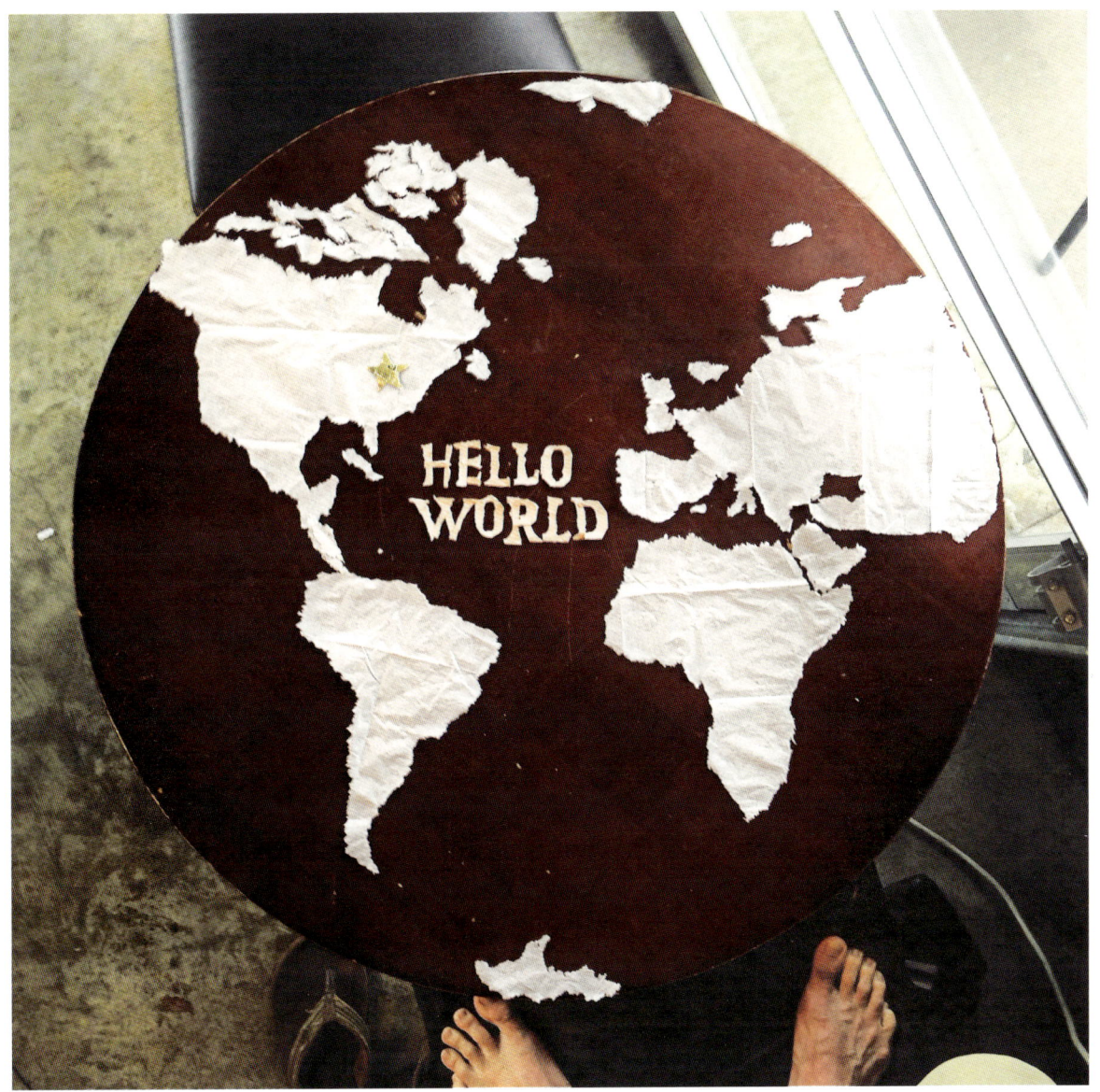

Hello World
Brian D. Parker, 2014

VENICE BEAT POET

I'm lost in Venice at night. Every wrong turn is interesting. Alleys lead to
smaller alleys that lead to tiny alleys that lead to huge alleys.

I step in a puddle. I only have one pair of shoes.

Three stories up, someone left their clothes on the line overnight.
All the other clotheslines are empty. I wonder if the neighbors complain.

Very late, I make it back to my room and sleep.

I wake early and sightsee. Later, exhausted, I take a nap on a bench facing the
Isola di Maggiore. I fall asleep too hard to be in public.

I'm roused by honking and banging and shouting. Italian curses echo off the stone
walls. It's a traffic jam—a boat traffic jam. Weird. Am I dreaming? A polizia boat comes.
I look to see if maybe Alan Funt or Fellini has cameras rolling.

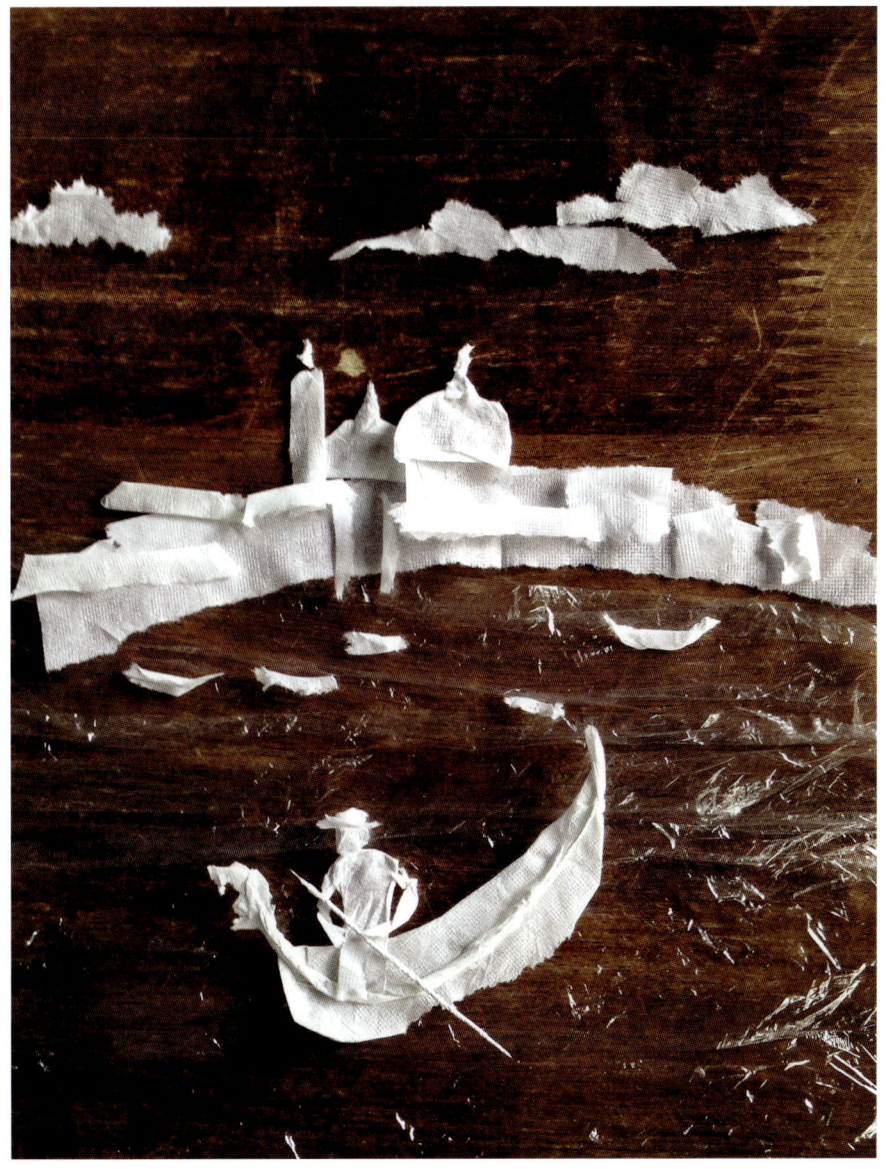

Venice
Brian D. Parker, 2014

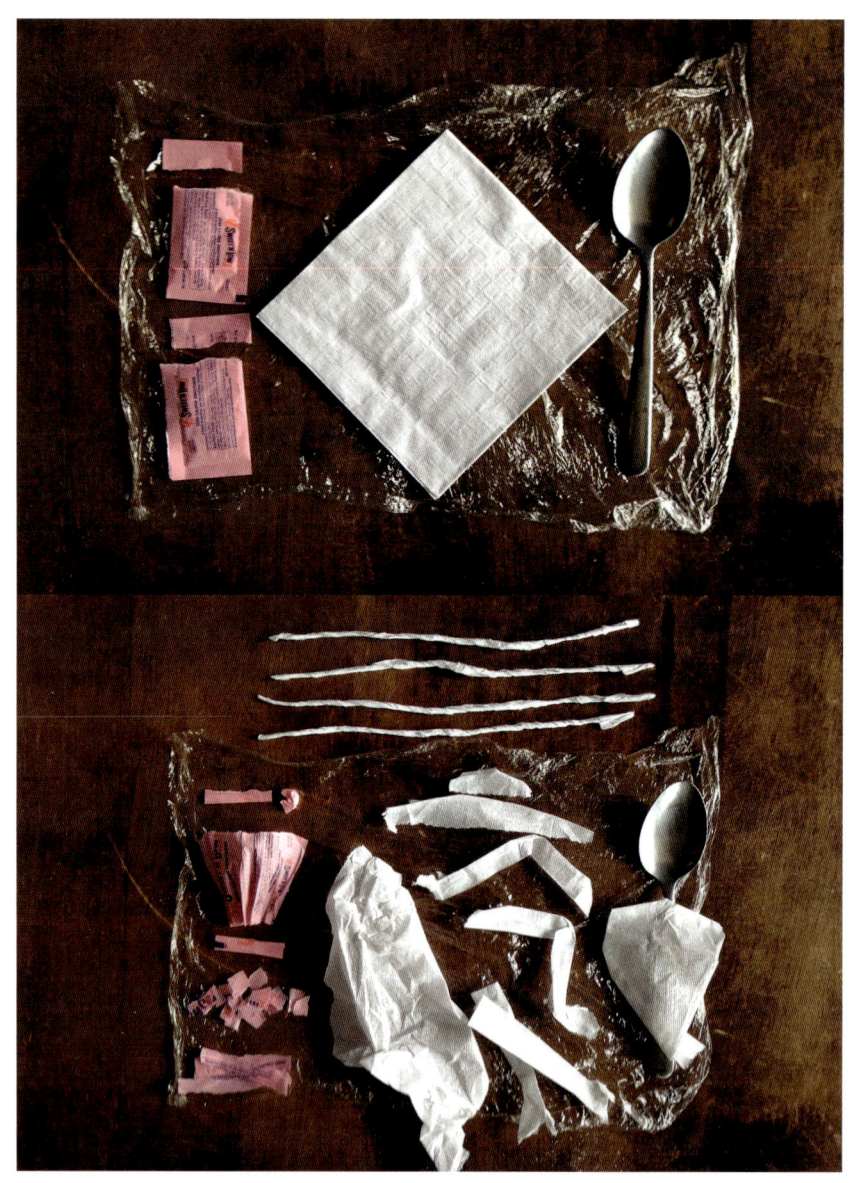

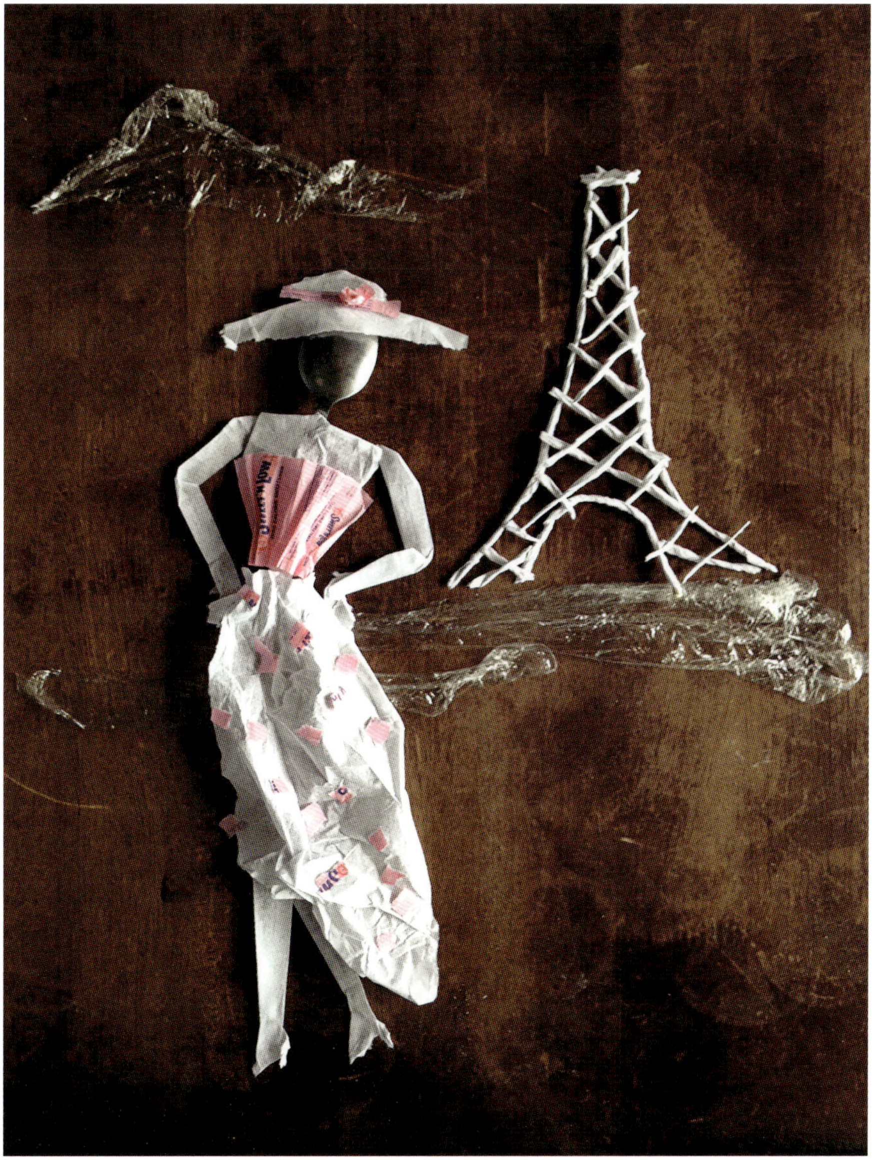

April in Paris
Brian D. Parker, 2014

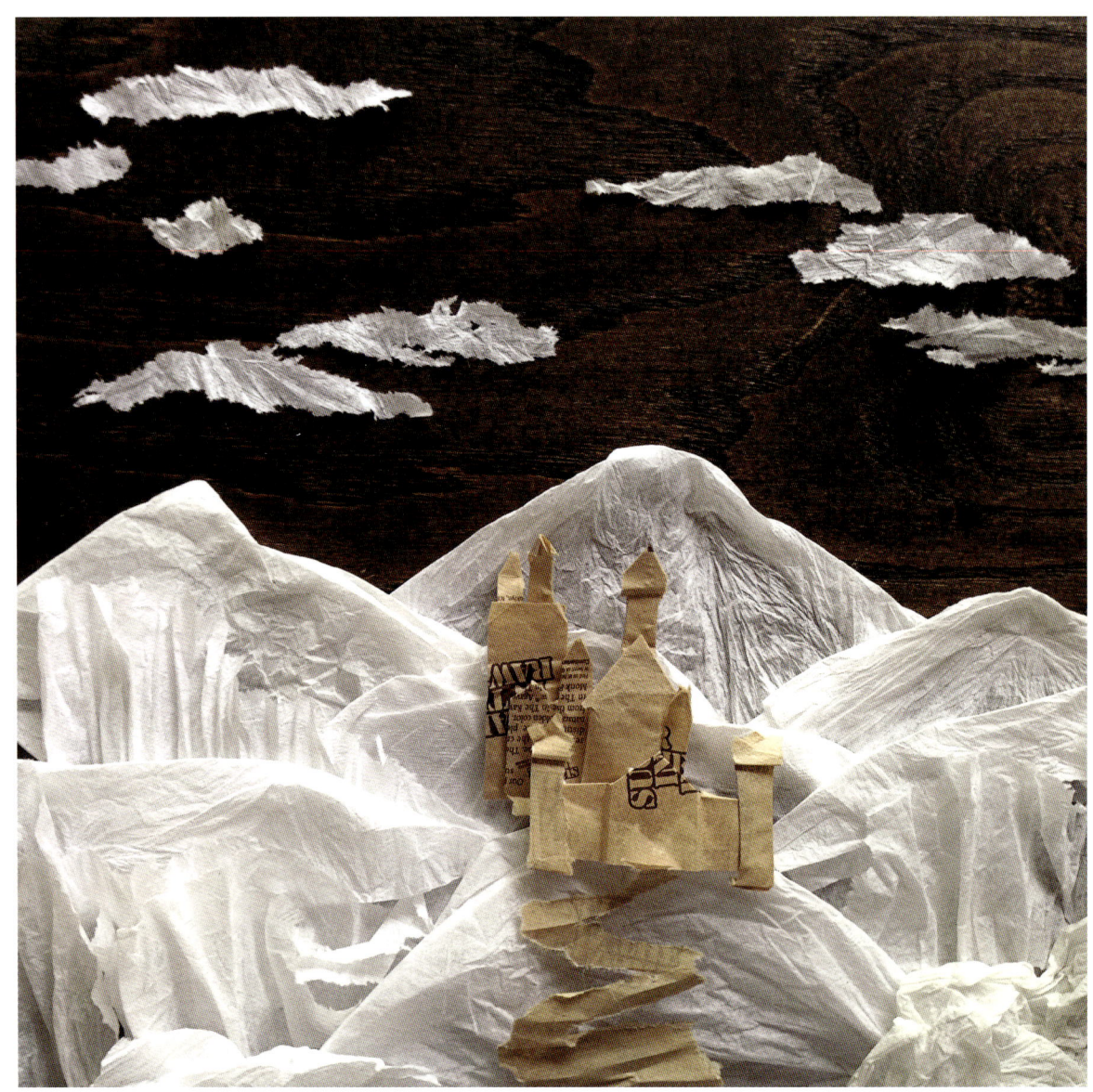

Neuschwanstein Castle
Brian D. Parker, 2014

NEW YORK NIGHT
(artwork on following page)

TEN THINGS I LOVE ABOUT MANHATTAN:

1. The absurdity of Times Square.

2. It's possible to see two different operas in one day. Once at the Met, I saw a matinee of Donizetti's L'elisir d'Amore," and, that evening, same stage, Franco Zeffirelli's production of Puccini's Tosca.

3. Almost anywhere, you can buy lime-green orchids at 3 a.m.

4. The Art Scene. It's just everywhere, and it's just outrageous.

5. The Parks. NYC is rich in charming public green spaces: from the tiniest verdant triangle to the grandiosity of Central Park.

6. The Ideas. New York is a swirling, out-of-control mass of compelling visions and thoughts.

7. The Theater Scene. Even on a Monday, you have bountiful choices.

8. The Grid. It's hard to get lost. Unlike most cities, the streets make sense.

9. The Skyline.

10. The Cheese, the cheese, the cheese.

New York Night (following page)
Brian D. Parker, 2014

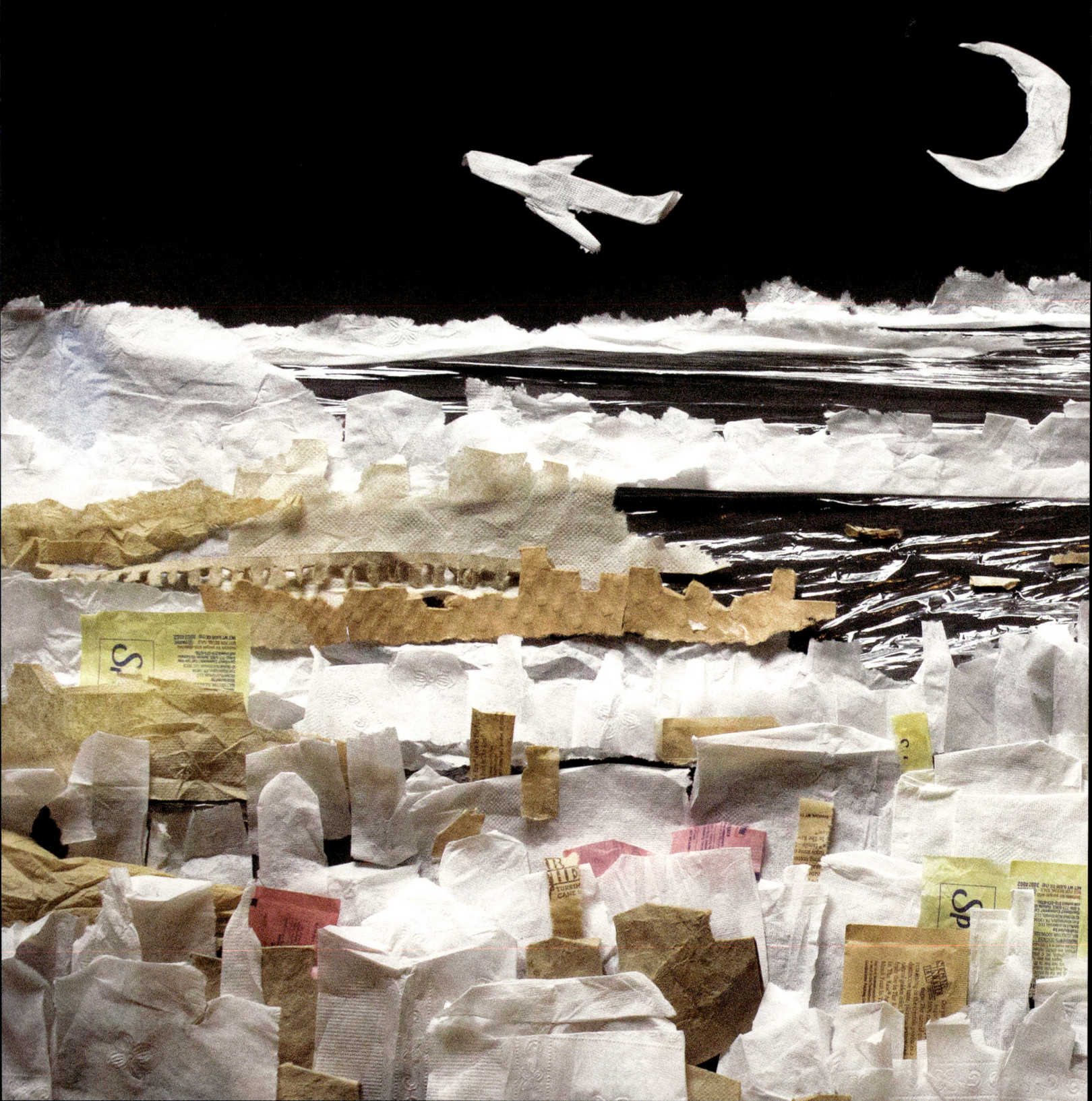

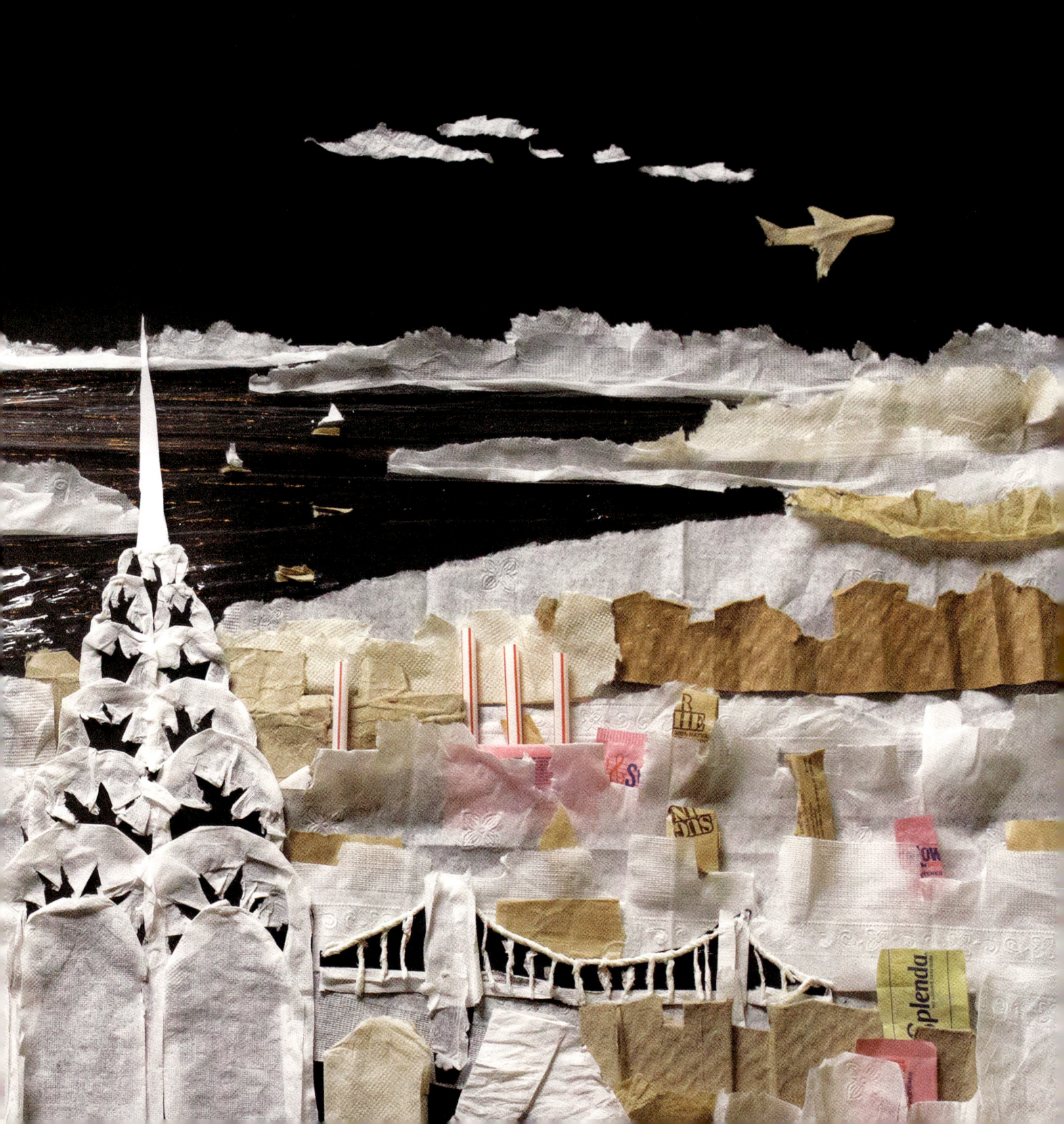

IN THE CROWN

I ran to the attendant and he closed the line behind me. I was the last person on Liberty Island to climb to the crown that day—the last day of my winter visit to New York.

I was surprised at the lack of finish inside the statue. This was the gritty underbelly of Lady Liberty—just open metal stairs snaking up through an intricate web of metal girding. It pleased me. I like to see how things work, and I was fascinated by the structure under the copper robes. The network of struts and supports seemed wild and haphazard. Thick, riveted ribs contoured the giant folds and shapes. Welded rods jutted and joined in unexpected points. It was a staggering amount of hand work.

I studied the precision of the ribs. Each one was probably hammered and re-hammered many times until the shape was perfect. I imagined a metal worker complaining about his boss, grumbling "T'will never be pleased," and "Flap-mouthed lout."

I looked up and realized I was being left behind. The last tourists were halfway to the crown and I was several flights below. I looked down wondering if a park ranger would soon follow me to clear the statue of visitors, but there was no one. I maintained my distance and continued up. When I was sure the crown was empty, I entered. The quiet was extaordinary, reverent. From this view, the Twin Towers were bigger than I thought. It was the only time I would see them in person. Their office lights had just started to shine in the dimming light. The December sun was pinking the sky. A boat, small from my height, crossed the waterway in slow motion. In a while, I would be down there too—on a different boat taking me back to the crowd. But for the moment, I surveyed lower Manhattan, proclaiming myself to be the most uniquely situated soul floating above a million other souls. And no one down there knew of me in my brief private loft.

I was pensive on the way down. I thought through tomorrow's travel details: checkout time, suitcases, taxi, the airport. And I then I remembered the present. I was still there. I was still in the Statue of Liberty all alone. I felt it for the full rare gift that it was. And even though my experience in the crown was over and already fading, I could still hold the magic of that moment. It was mine. And I knew some of that magic would always stay with me.

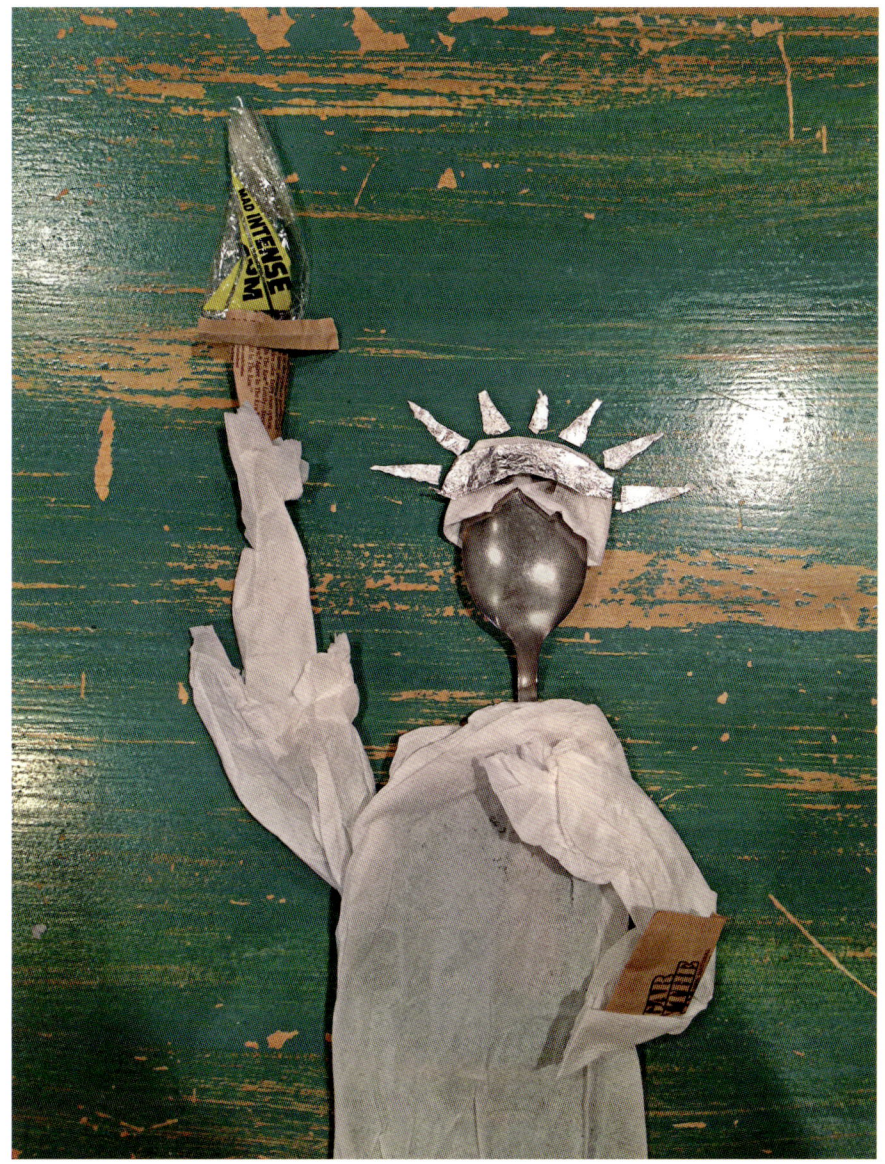

Lady Liberty
Brian D. Parker, 2014

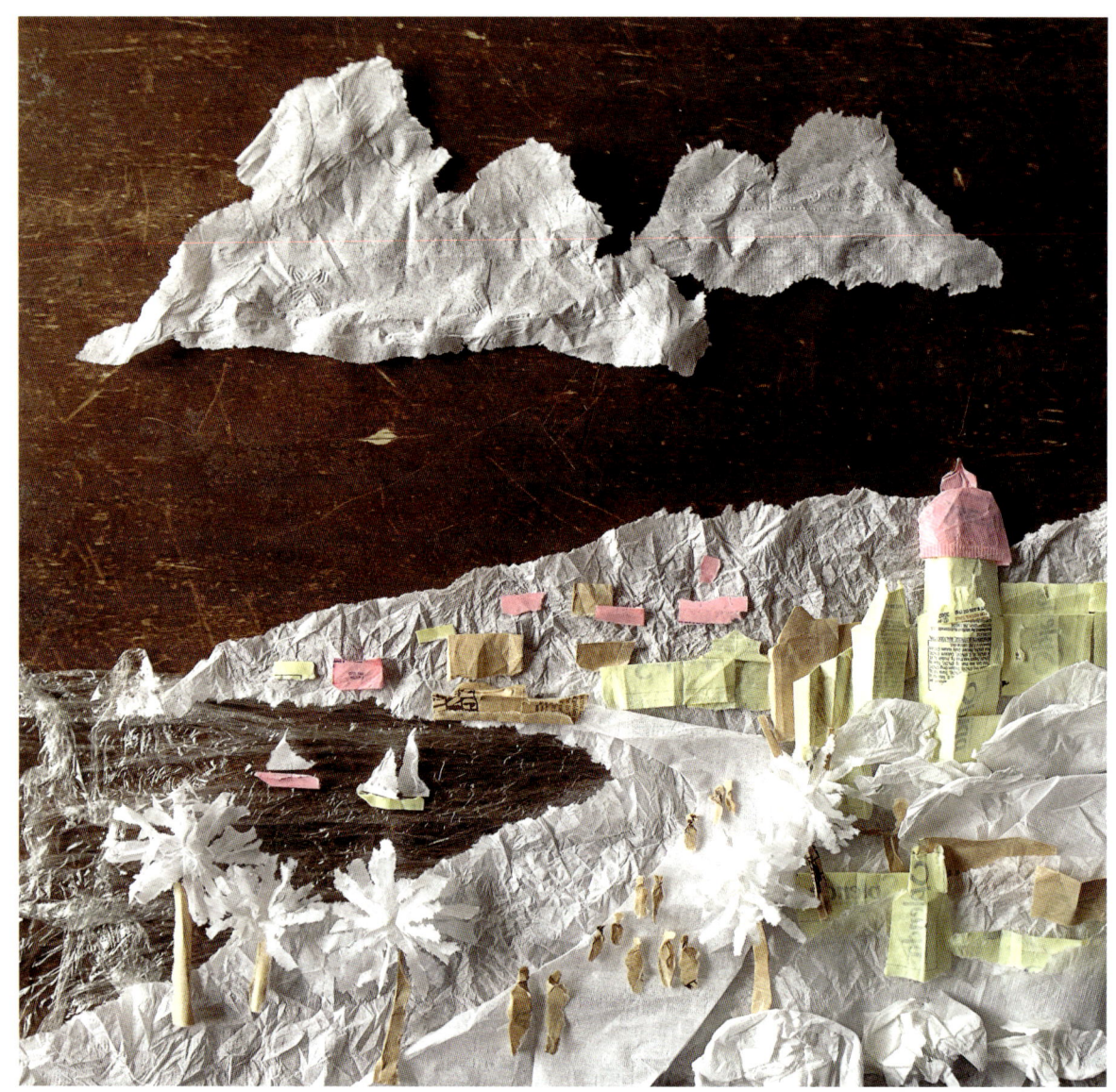

Nice, France
Brian D. Parker, 2014

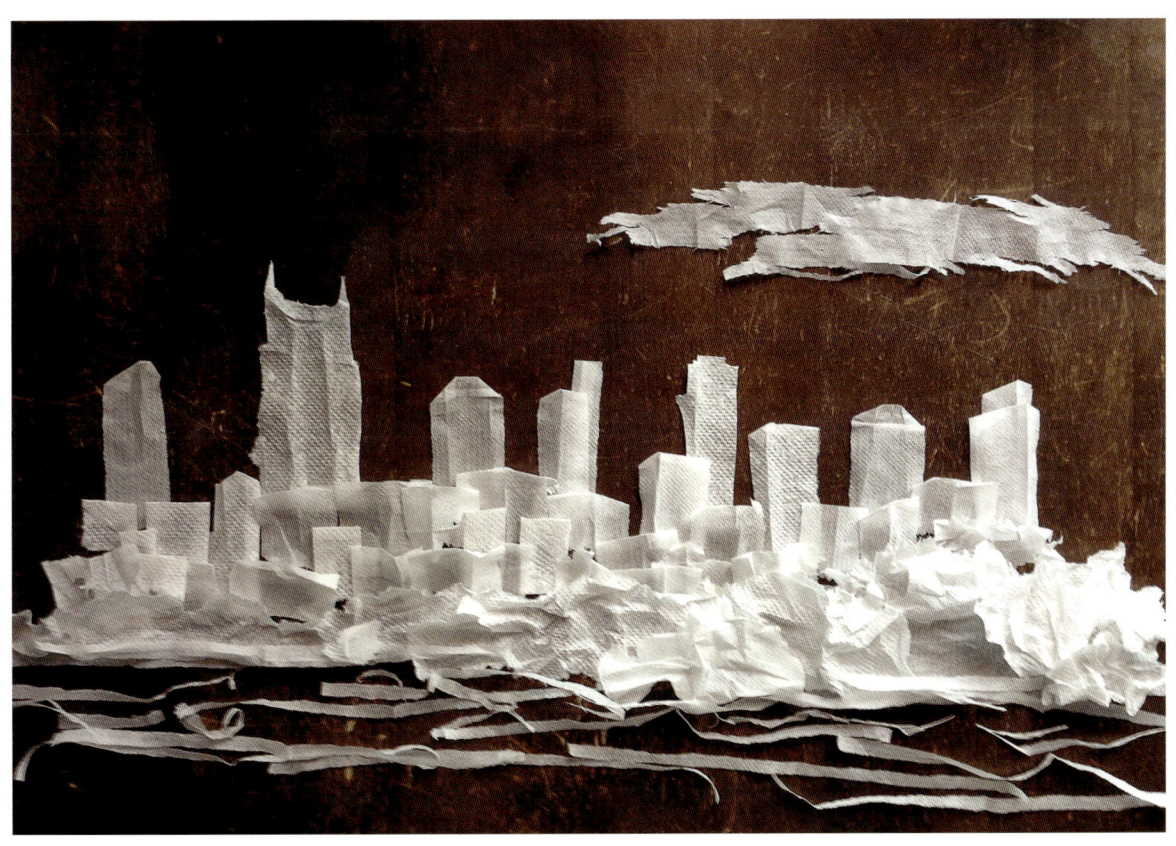

Nashville Skyline
Brian D. Parker, 2014

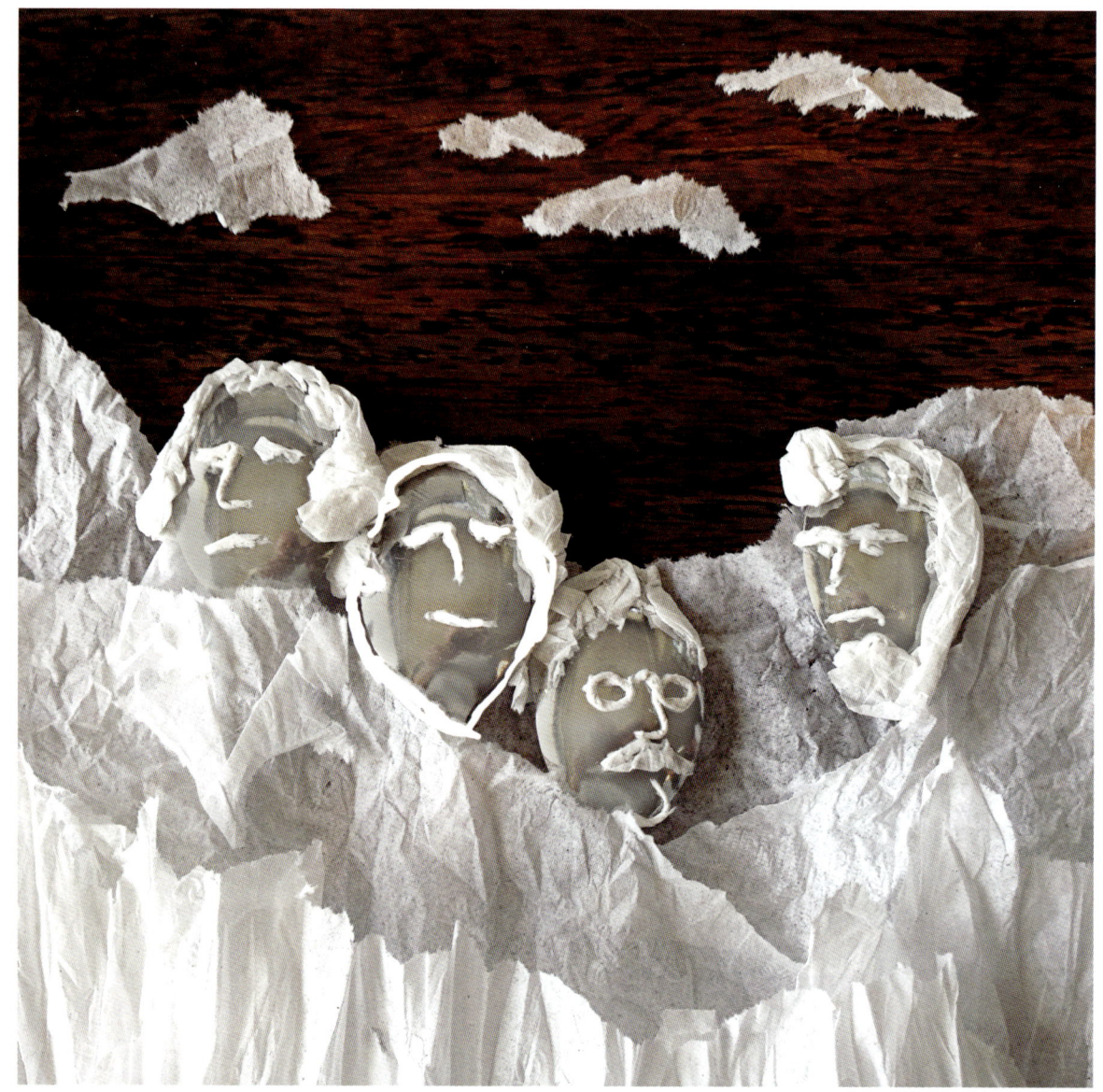

Mount Rushmore
Brian D. Parker, 2014

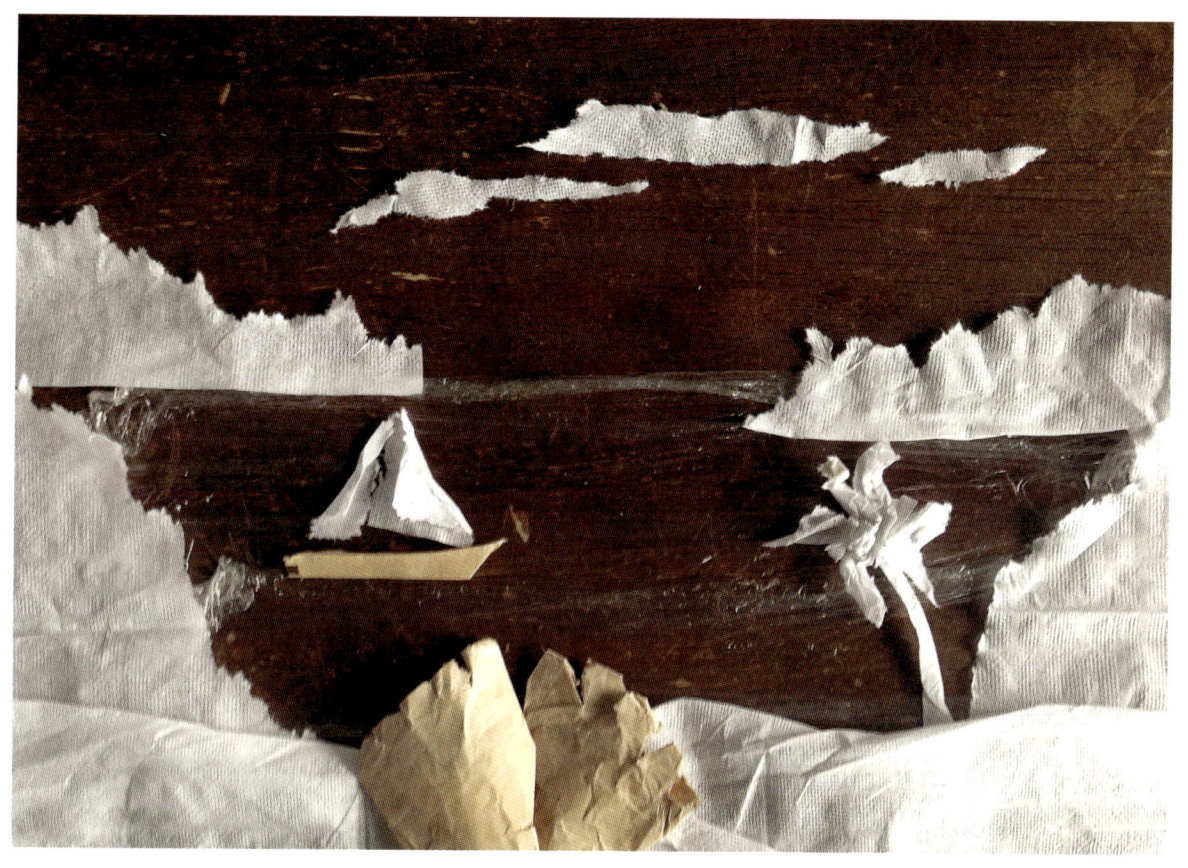

Brown Toes in Hawaii
Brian D. Parker, 2014

MOJAVE COYOTE

I am no expert on desert crossings, but I have traversed the arid west probably a dozen times. Hmm? Maybe ten. Anyway, I have a little advice in matters of the Mojave and it bears sharing:

1. Check your spare tire before you leave.

2. Never let your gas gauge get below a quarter tank.

3. Go see the Wigwam Motel in San Bernardino, California.

4. Go see the dinosaurs in Cabazon, California.

5. Spend an afternoon at Mojave National Preserve and/or Joshua Tree National Preserve.

6. If you don't have air conditioning in your car, don't cross the desert.

7. If you cross the desert anyway, wear SPF30 sunblock on your left arm.

8. If you cross the desert anyway, clothing is optional.

9. If you cross the desert anyway, don't use a fake fur seat cover. They are very absorbent.

10. If you cross the desert anyway, and do use a fake fur seat cover . . . just don't. Don't do it.

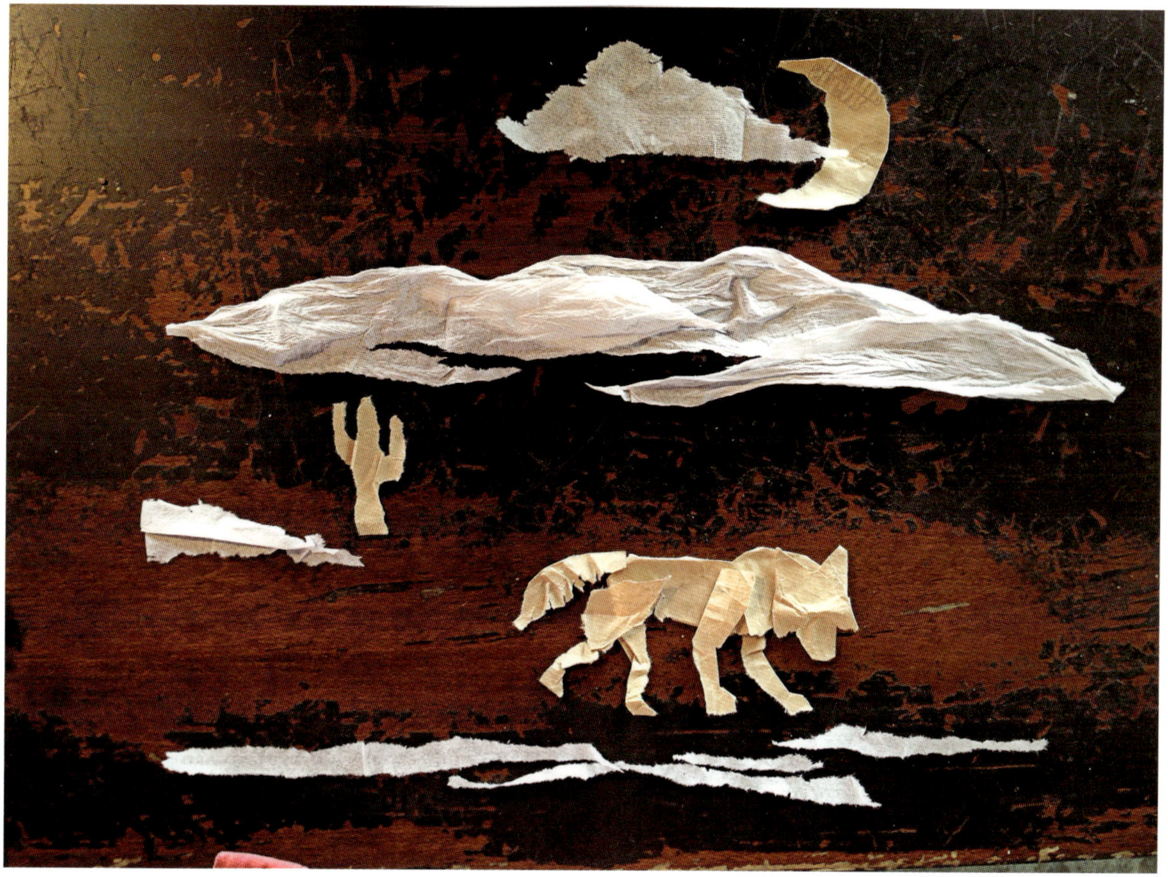

Mojave Coyote
Brian D. Parker, 2014

CAMPING IN NEW ENGLAND

Donna Reedy was a strong New England woman. Her daughter, Lisa, and I were good friends—friends from early Sunday school days. The summer of my high school graduation, Donna took a few of us camping to the northeastern states that she loved. It is one of my favorite memories. Lisa, Ethan (Lisa's brother), Andy, Jeff, and I boarded her old pickup camper and drove out of the Midwestern cornfields to New England. I was in the cab with Donna when she decided to have a heart to heart with me about my future—something I hadn't really thought about beyond college. It was a good, meaningful talk and a good, meaningful trip. Decades have passed and the memory is still strong.

Just a few days before Donna died, she asked me to create a napkin art piece for her. I knew exactly what to make. "Camping in New England" was my gift for her. Although she has passed on, I know it stays with her just as her gifts have stayed with me. I still feel them in big and small ways. Here are a few:

Donna introduced me to the greatest sandwich on earth—the lobster roll.

She was a wild woman on the piano. Donna could play the fire out of a camp meeting hymn.

She introduced me to the rich beauty of New England.

She told me how to pick out a good wool sweater.

She introduced me to shrimp dip: Campbell's Cream of Shrimp soup, cream cheese, and scallions. Delicious with Hawaiian bread and Lactaid.

She taught me to turn on the heater if the car engine overheats.

She told me to be intentional with my life.

She taught me how to love the ocean.

Thank you, Donna Reedy.

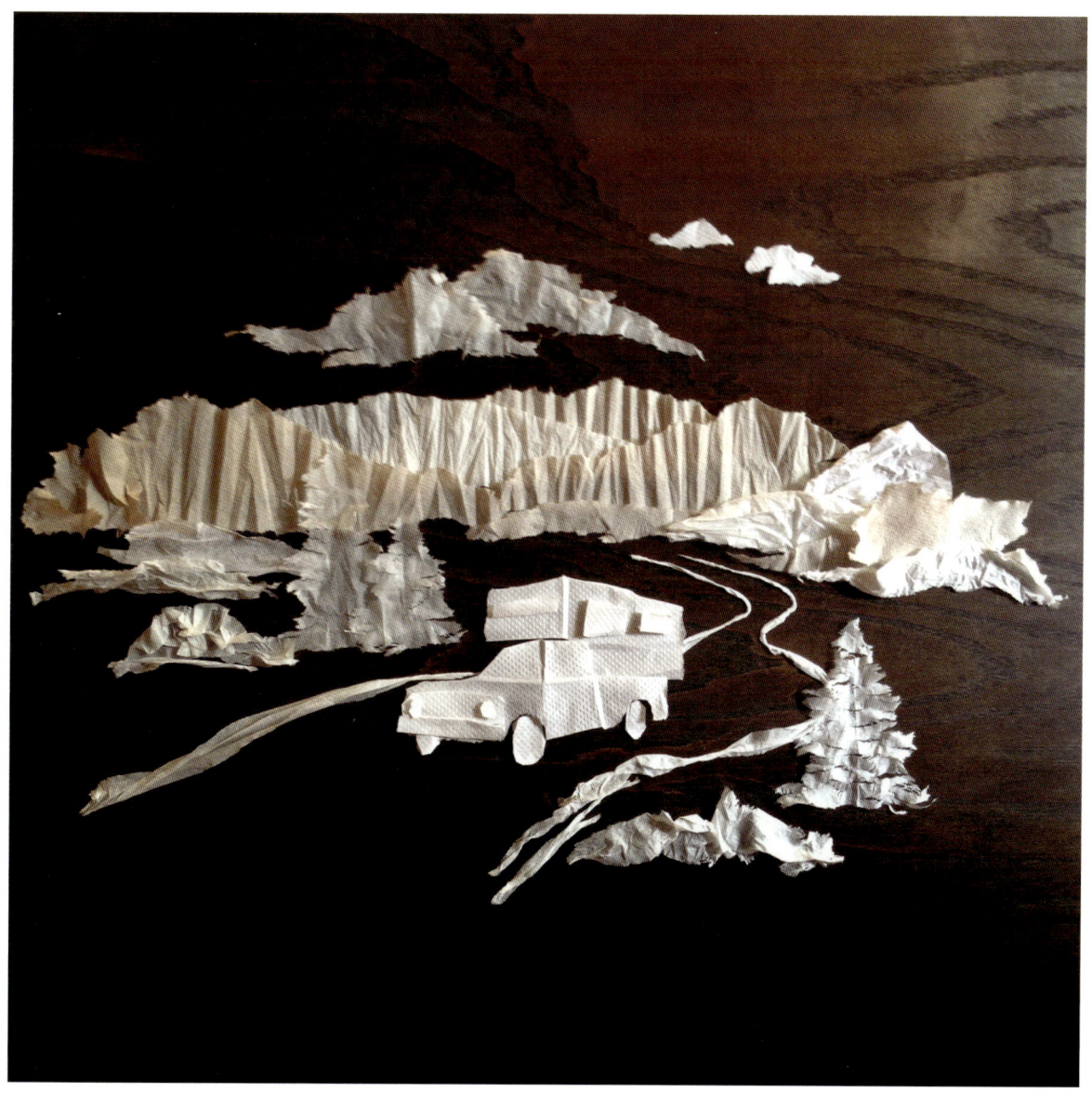

Camping in New England
Brian D. Parker, 2014

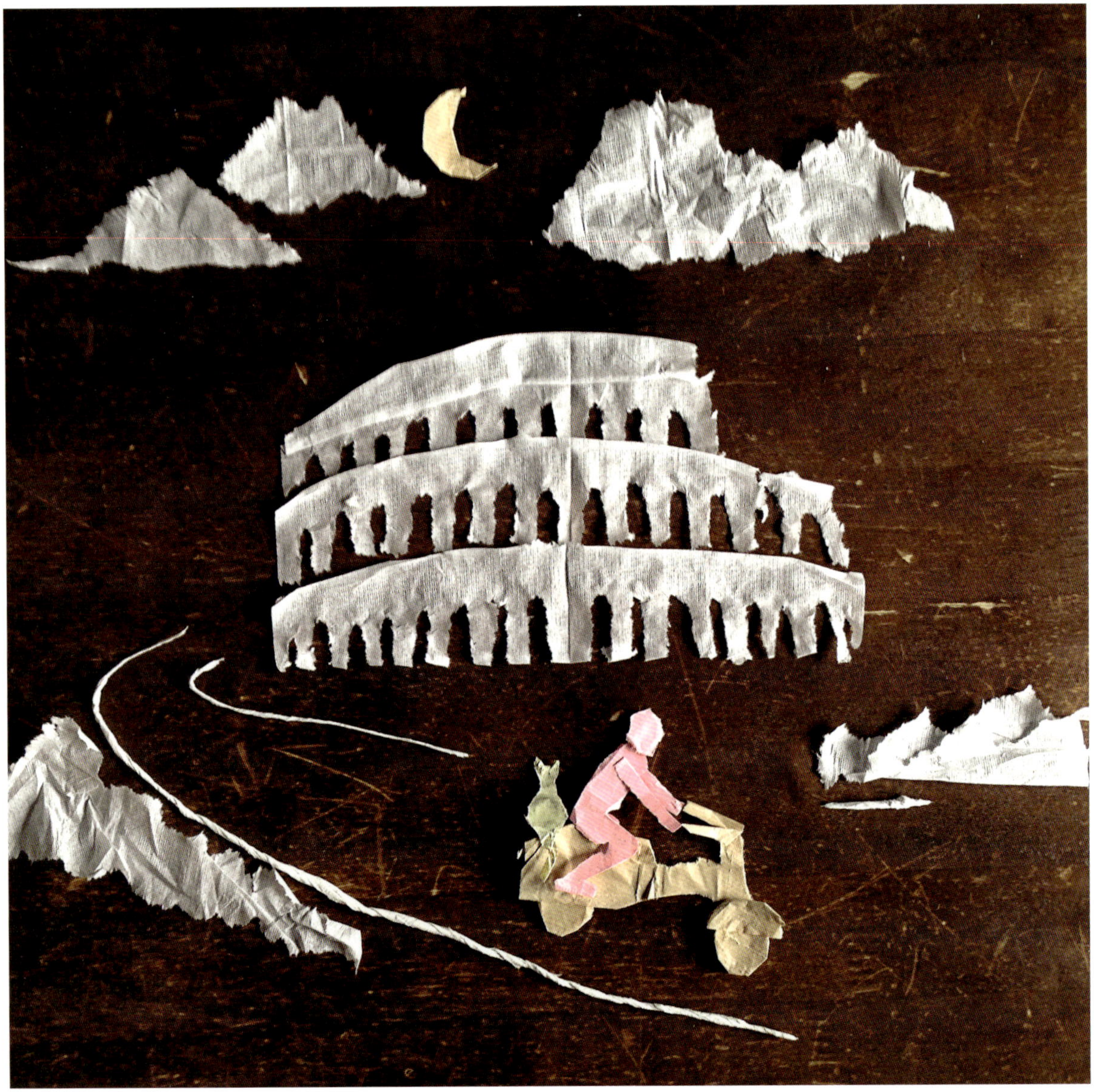

Rome
Brian D. Parker, 2014

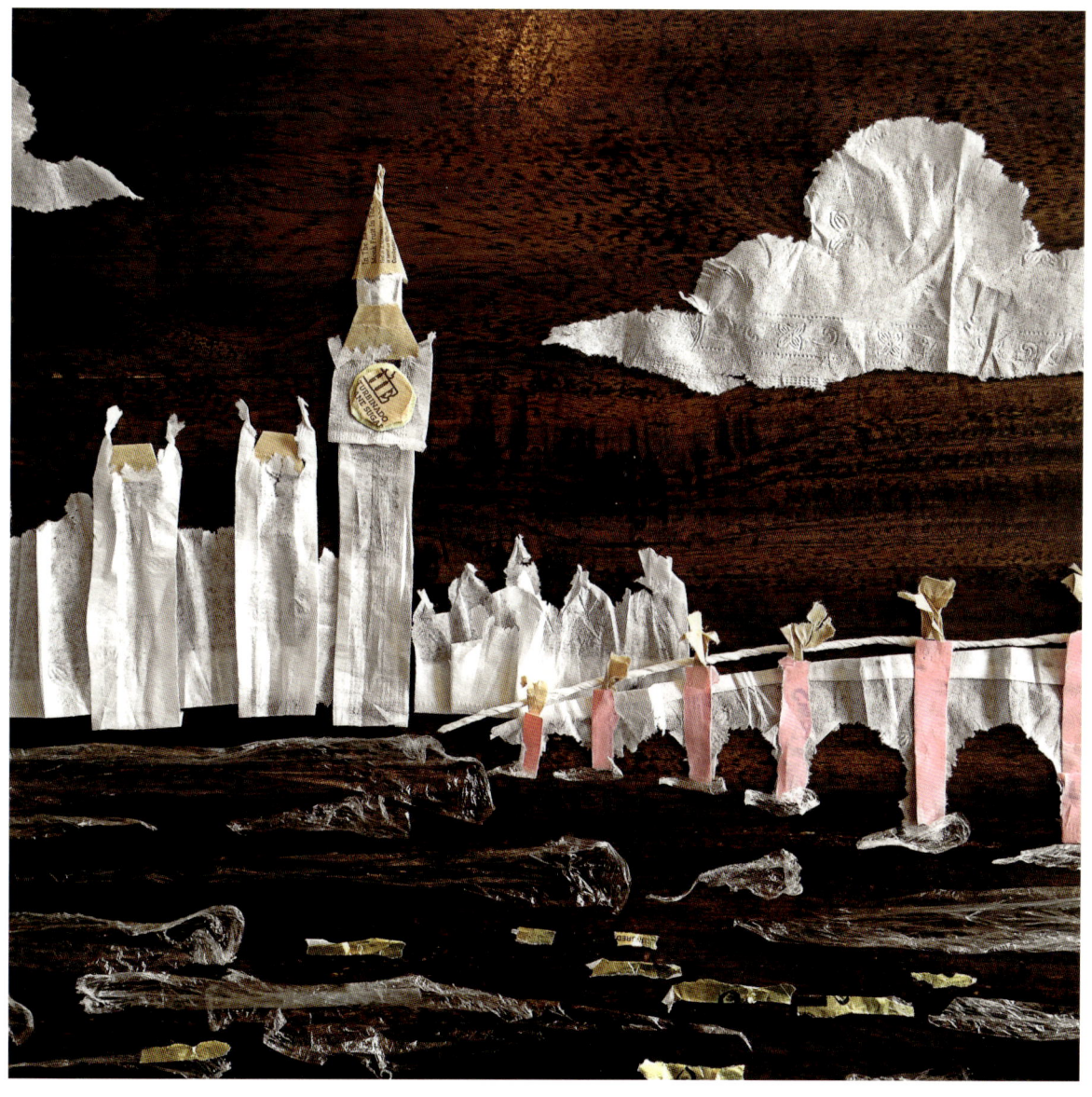

London
Brian D. Parker, 2014

PORTBOU
(artwork on page 67)

It was late at night and the mean-looking guys kept their hands in their coat pockets. They were making me nervous. About 5 benches away, the three of them huddled together, whispering and glancing at the three of us. Our train was very late. We were young, scared, and we didn't know anything about Portbou, Spain.

I was traveling with friends from Paris to Barcelona. The train track size changed at the French-Spanish border, so we had to switch railroads at Portbou. The train to Barcelona, however, had yet to arrive. I was worried

The lights were still on in the train station, but the employees had just left and we were alone with the mean guys. We decided to go somewhere, anywhere away from them. Very casually, we walked through the station and saw a pedestrian tunnel. I tried not to but I looked back. They were following. The tunnel was dark and unknown, but it seemed the best option. In fact, it was the only escape at that point. Still casual, we trotted down the stairs and then I heard their footsteps speeding. We came to a "T" in the tunnel. Left or right? We turned right and ran. Just as I heard them round the corner, there it was: the light at the end of the tunnel. They stopped, and we kept running full speed onto a lantern-lined cobblestone street. I wanted to find help—the policía, anyone. No luck. The street was empty. But the moon was high, and it seemed that the mean guys were unwilling to follow us outside. The relief was crushing. Civilization was asleep, but nearby, if they came back.

I stopped to catch my breath and look around. The street was beautiful—almost Disney-esque: a Thomas Kincaid painting of a quaint Spanish village. Colorful planters and baskets peppered the sidewalk along the shuttered stucco buildings. Flowering vines climbed the walls. The atmosphere was so charming, it was jarring. Just moments ago, I was being pursued by muggers, and now I felt like I was sneaking around Adventureland after hours. We paused and looked back at the tunnel exit—now small and distant. Best of all, there was no sign of threat. We walked downhill and I could hear the sounds of the bay. A little further and there were boats and a few people. We didn't have a plan, but now we felt safe.

A fisherman directed us to the nearest hotel, the Casa La Masia. It was a simple, lovely hotel with thick, white walls and a large tree trunk growing up through the lobby. I liked it immediately. The only problem was that we hadn't changed currency and the banks were closed. Would they let us stay on credit? All we could do is hope for mercy. I rang the bell and an old man, grumpy and tousled, stumbled out from the doorway. It didn't look good for us. I was already bracing myself for a cold fitful sleep on the pier.

In broken Spanish, I pled our case. I offered him our passports as collateral and promised we would "cambie los dólares mañana." His face changed and he smiled. He consented and showed us to our rooms. I lay down and sighed with relief. It had been a long, harrowing day in a strange country. Even if Bradley, Illinois was more than an ocean away, I'd never felt so safe and at home.

That was many years ago. But I still have a comb from Casa La Masia. Once a year, I dig it out, hang it on my Christmas tree, and remember the fear and the relief. I feel it all over again. And I remember that any place with a smile can feel like home.

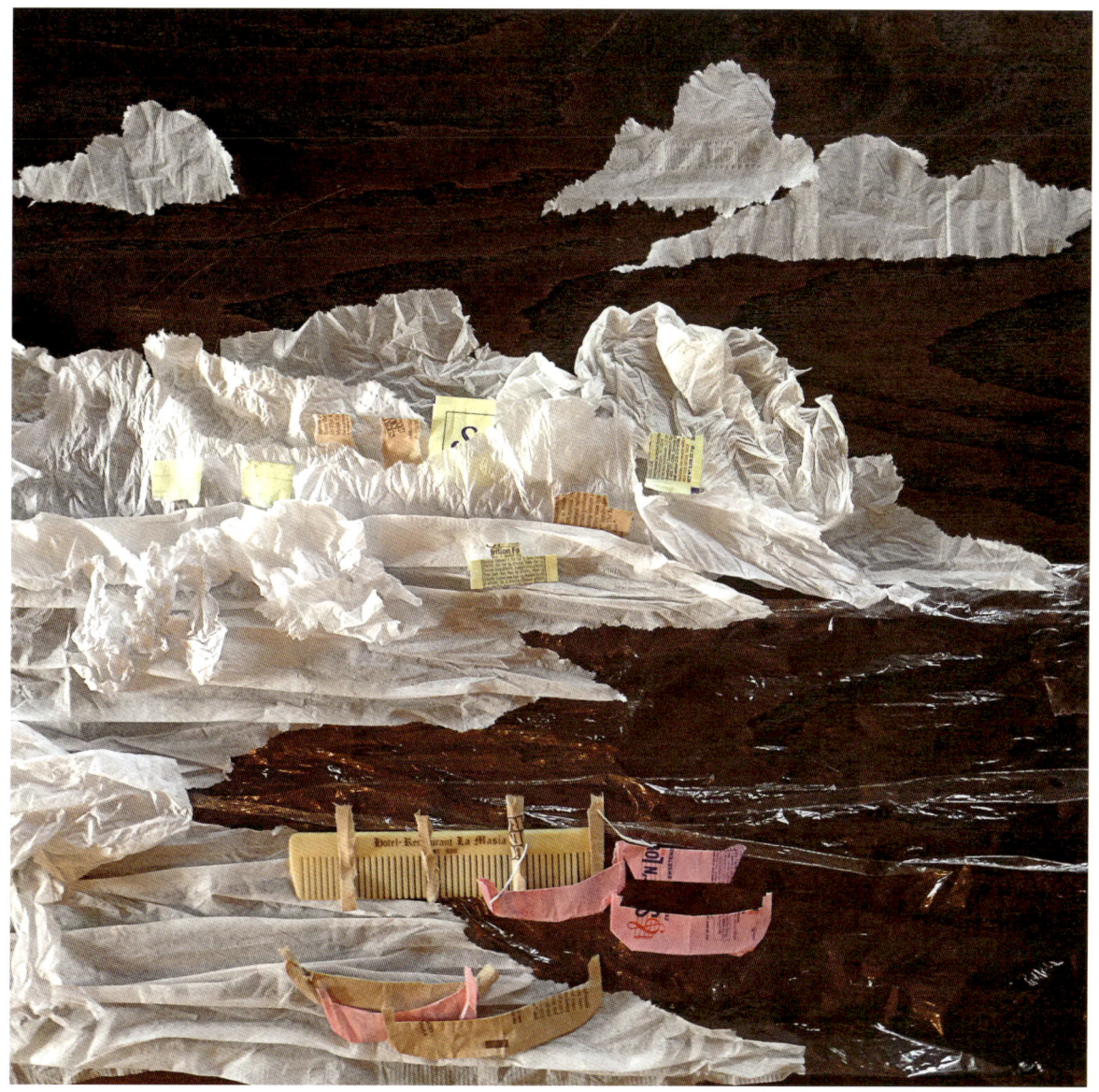

Portbou
Brian D. Parker, 2014

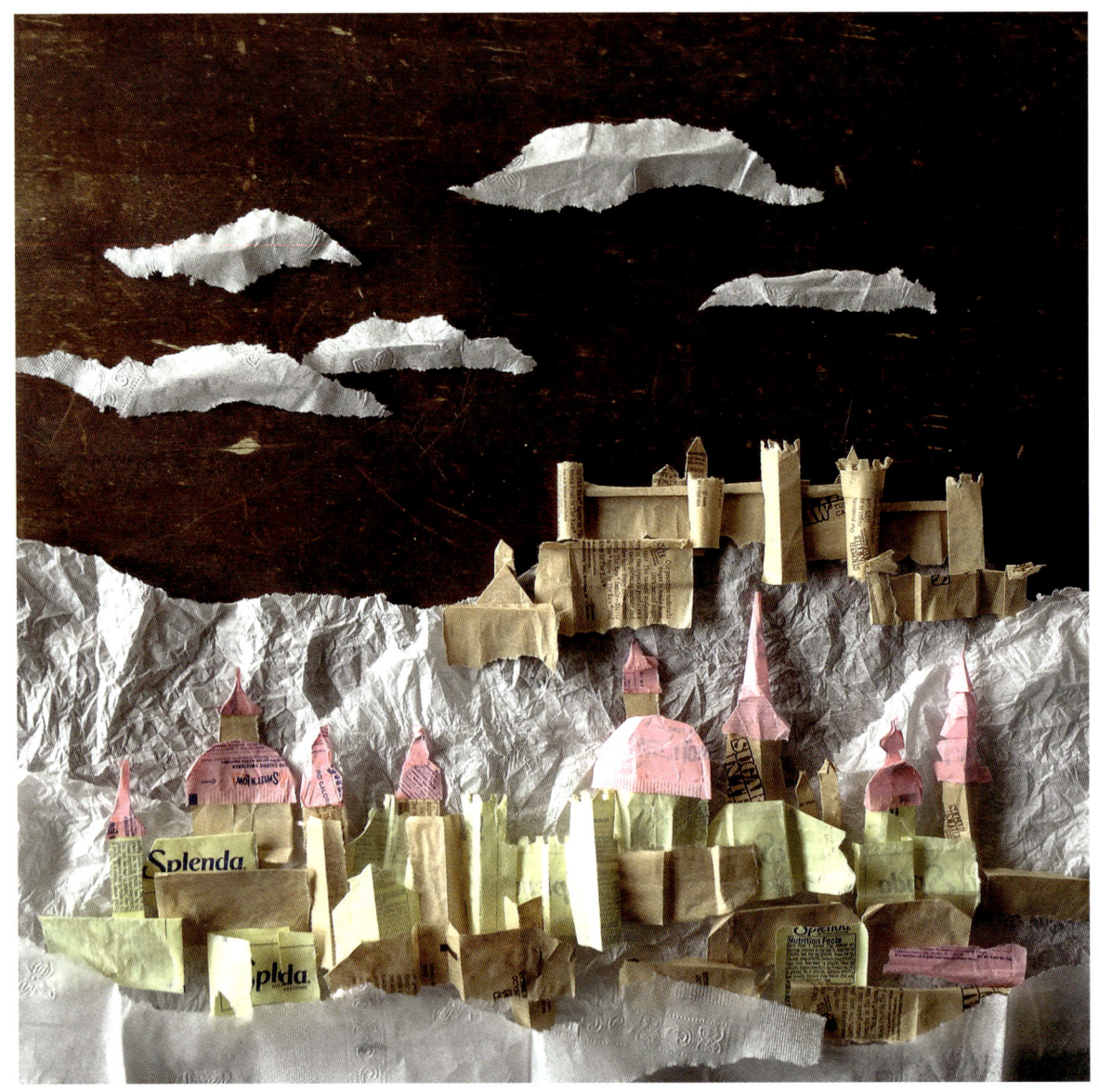

Salzburg, Austria
Brian D. Parker, 2014

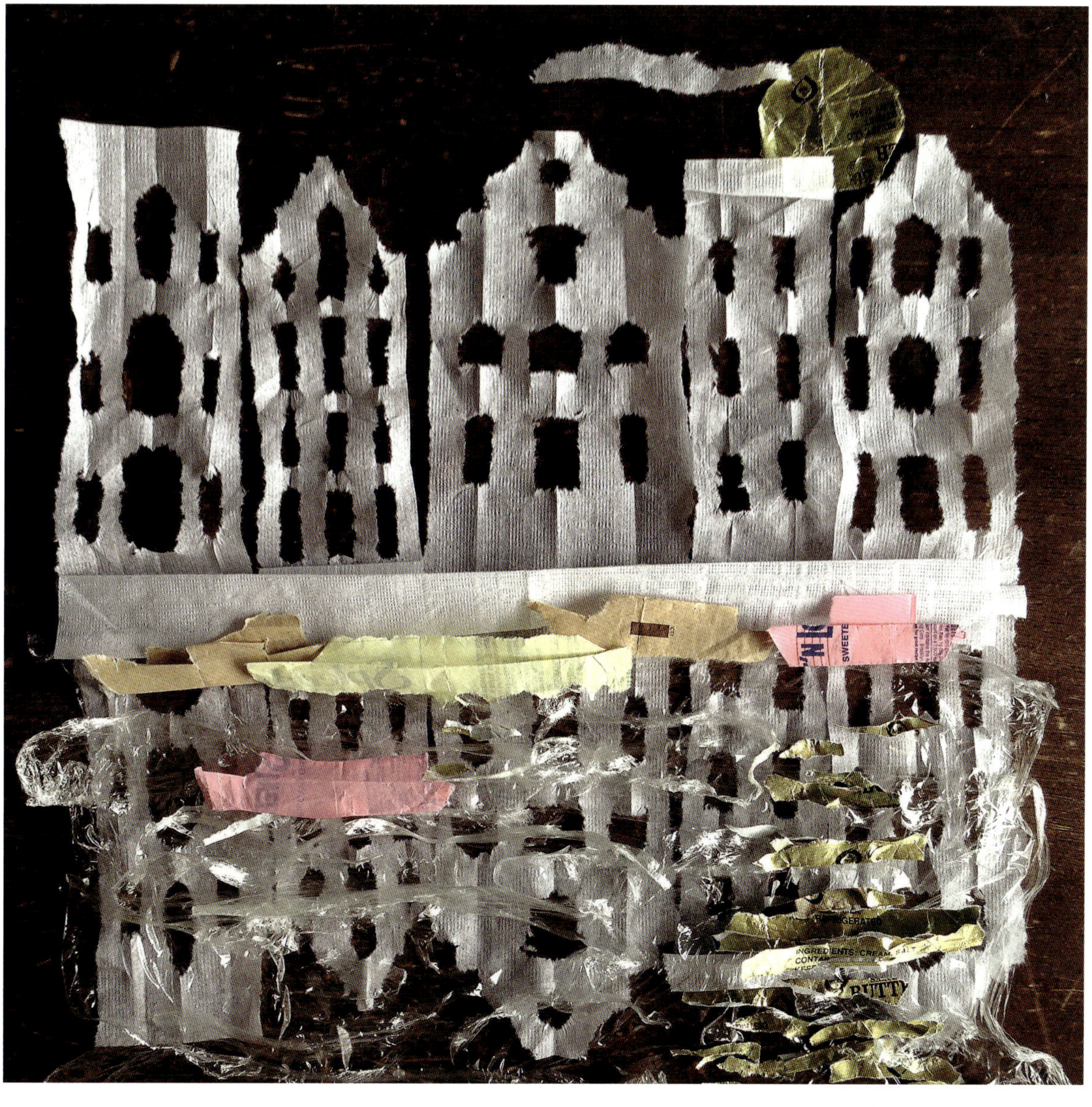

Amsterdam, Netherlands
Brian D. Parker, 2014

THE SEASONS

A Collection Inspired by the Passing Year

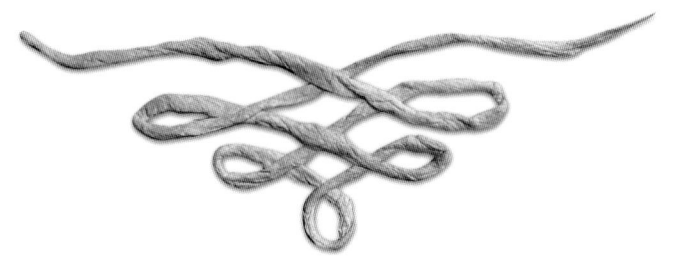

SPRING

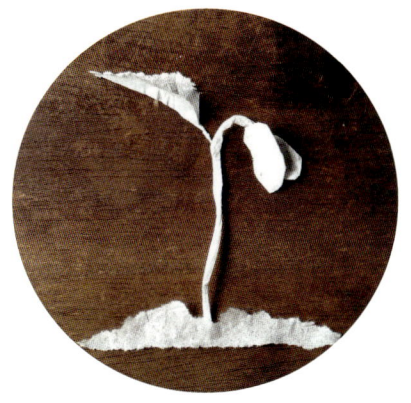

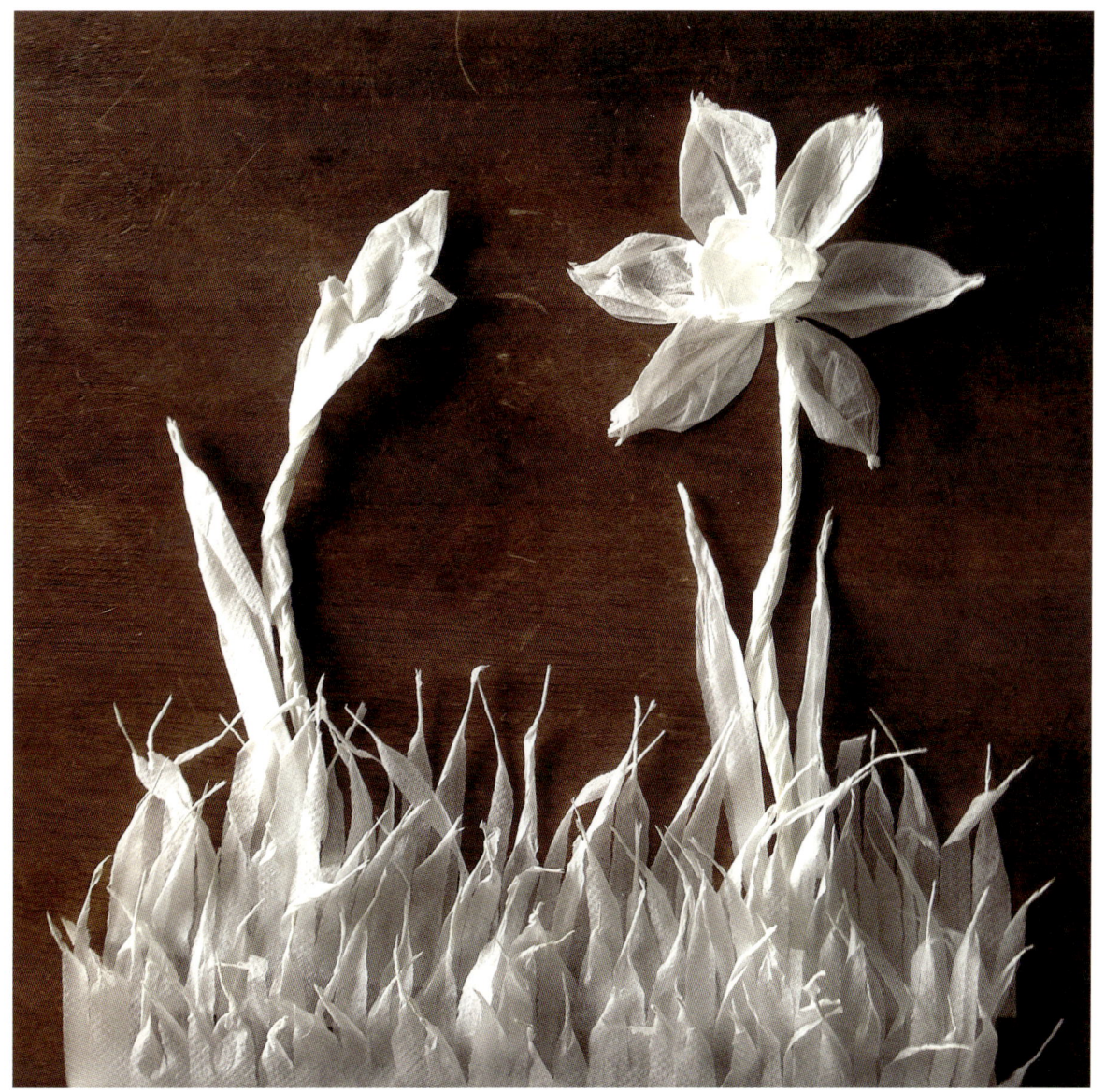

Daffodils
Brian D. Parker, 2014

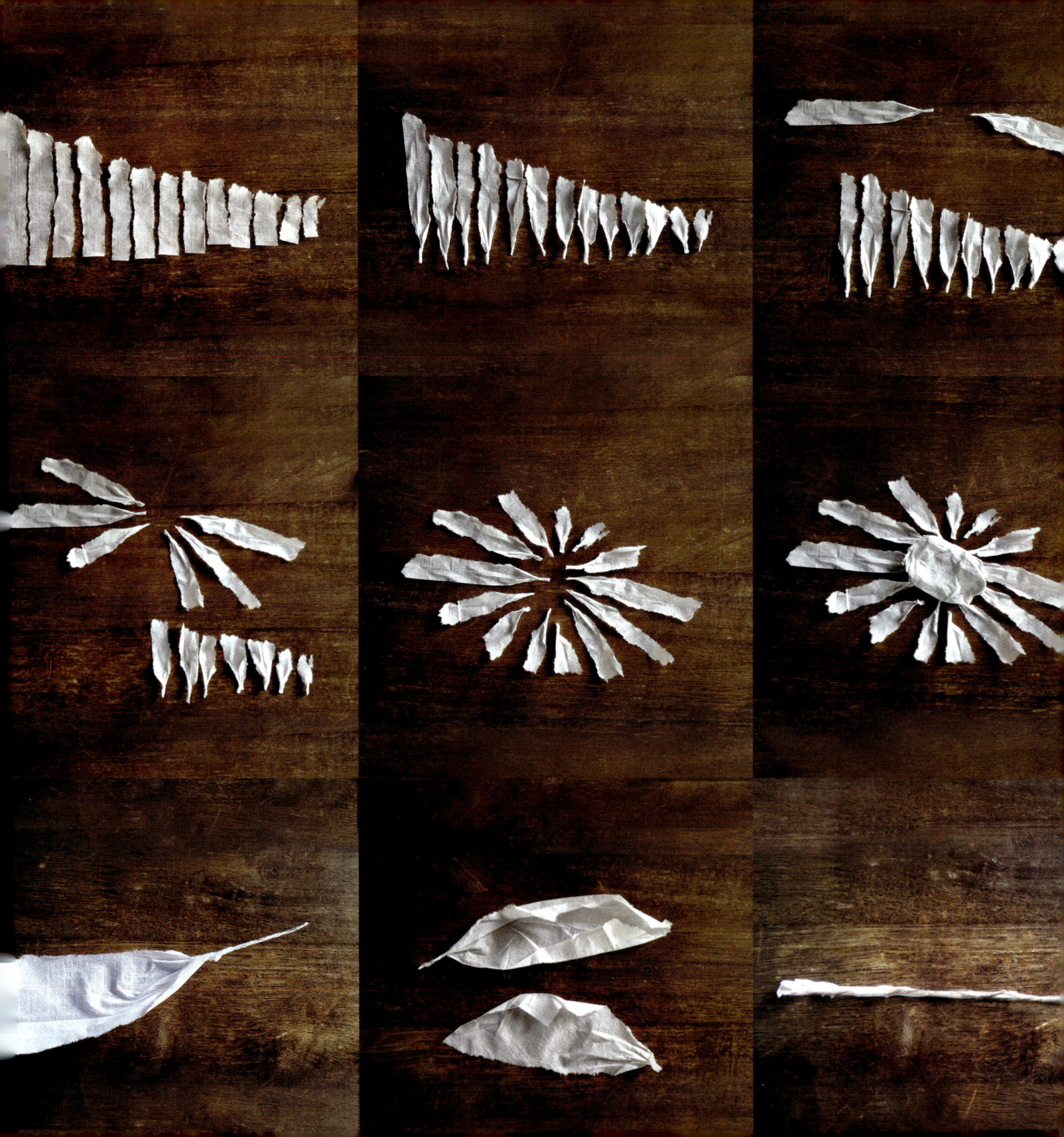

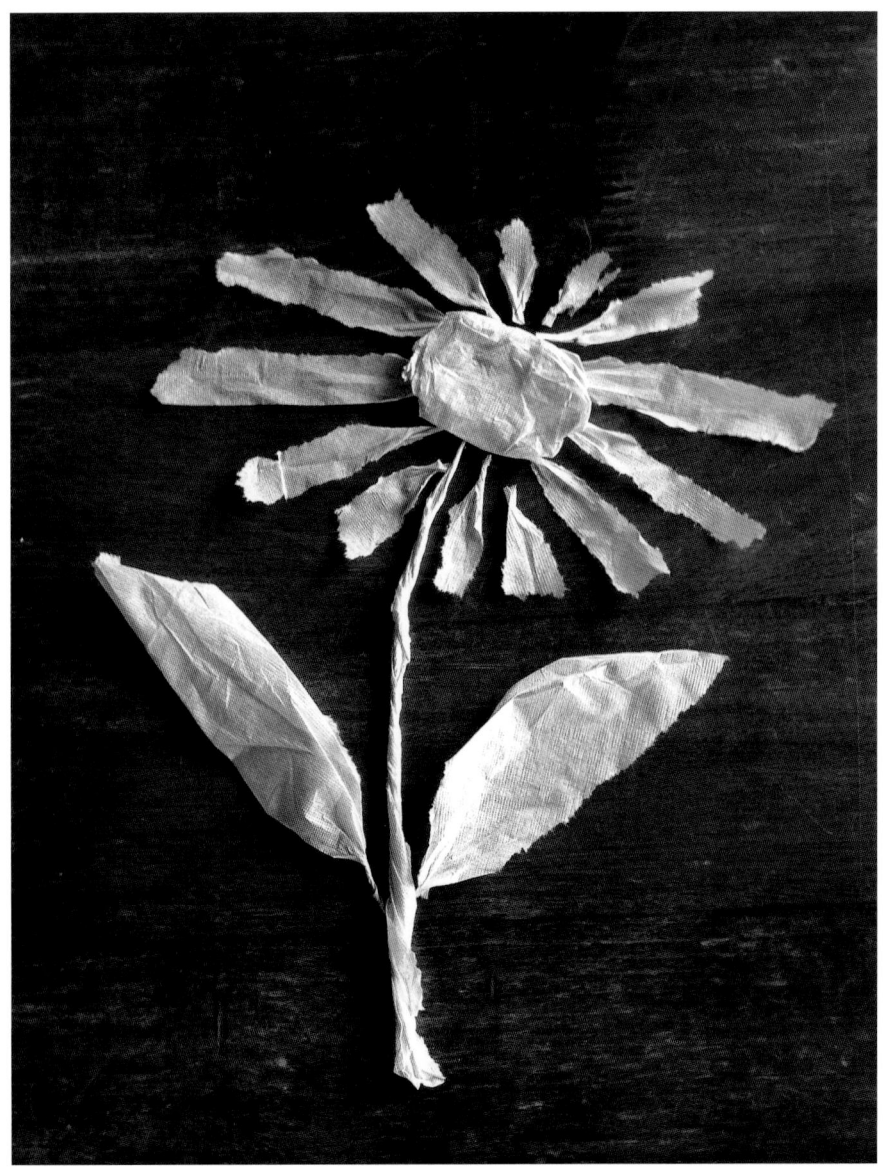

Simple Flower
Brian D. Parker, 2014

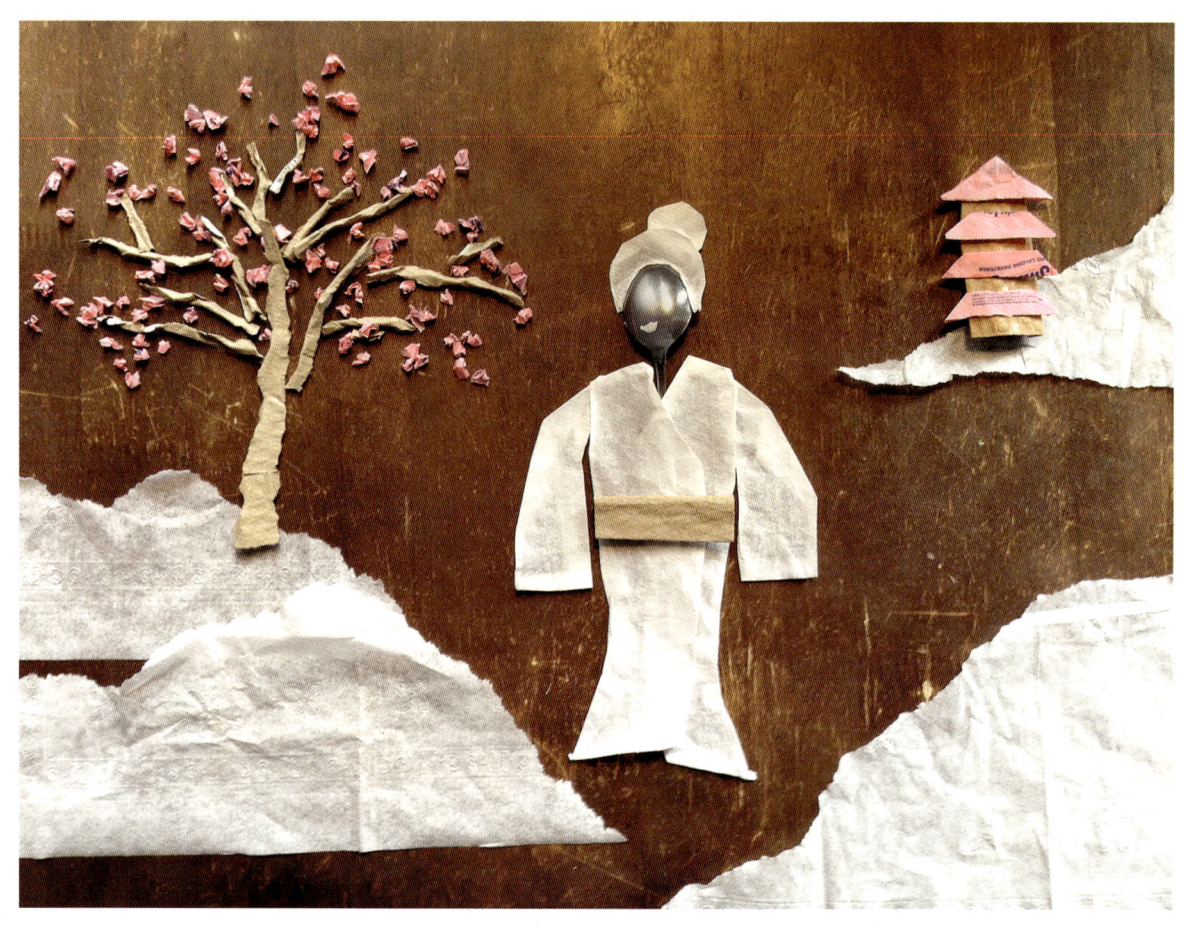

Spring Kimono
Brian D. Parker, 2014

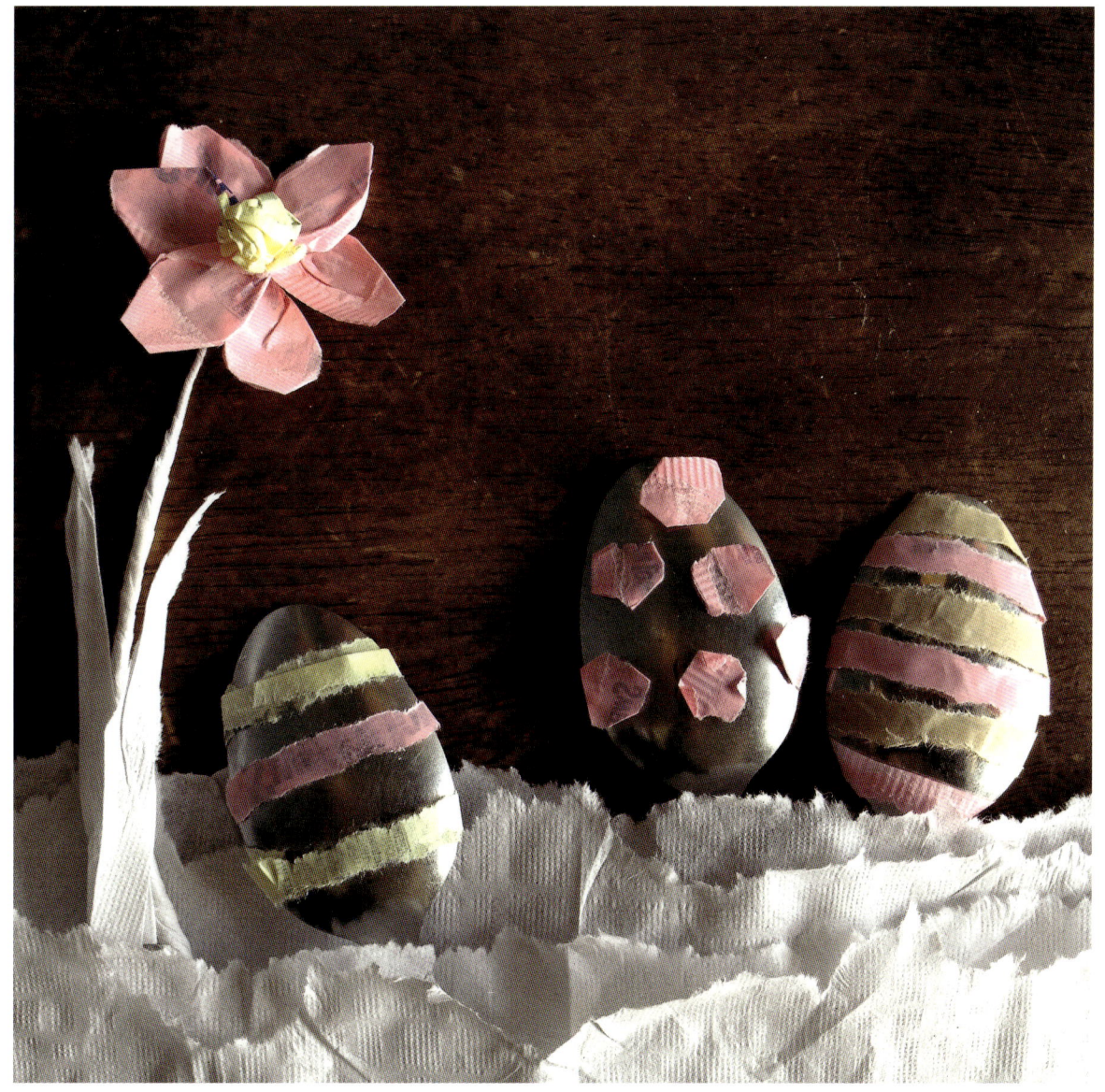

Easter Eggs
Brian D. Parker, 2014

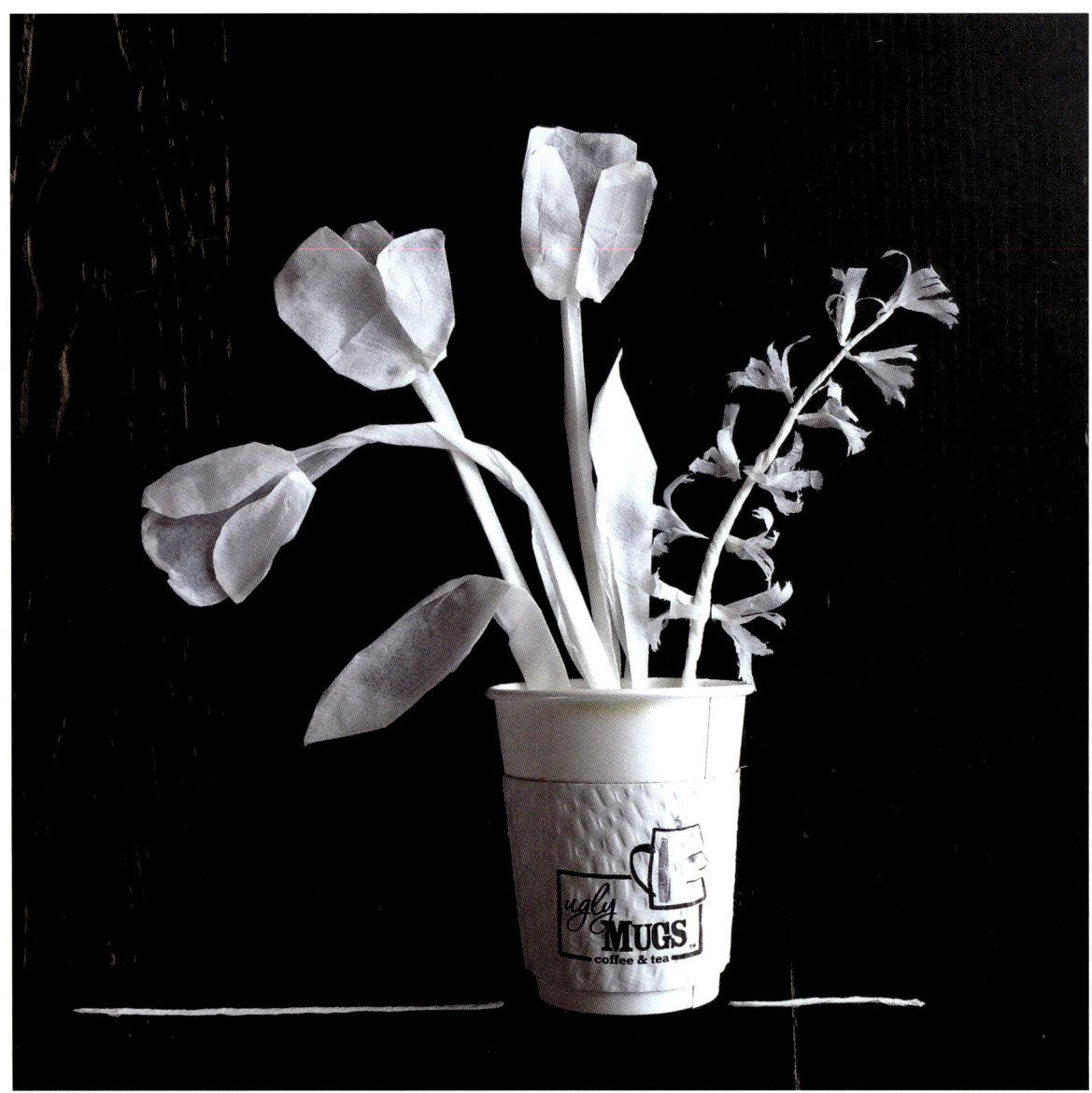

Tulips and Forsythia
Brian D. Parker, 2014

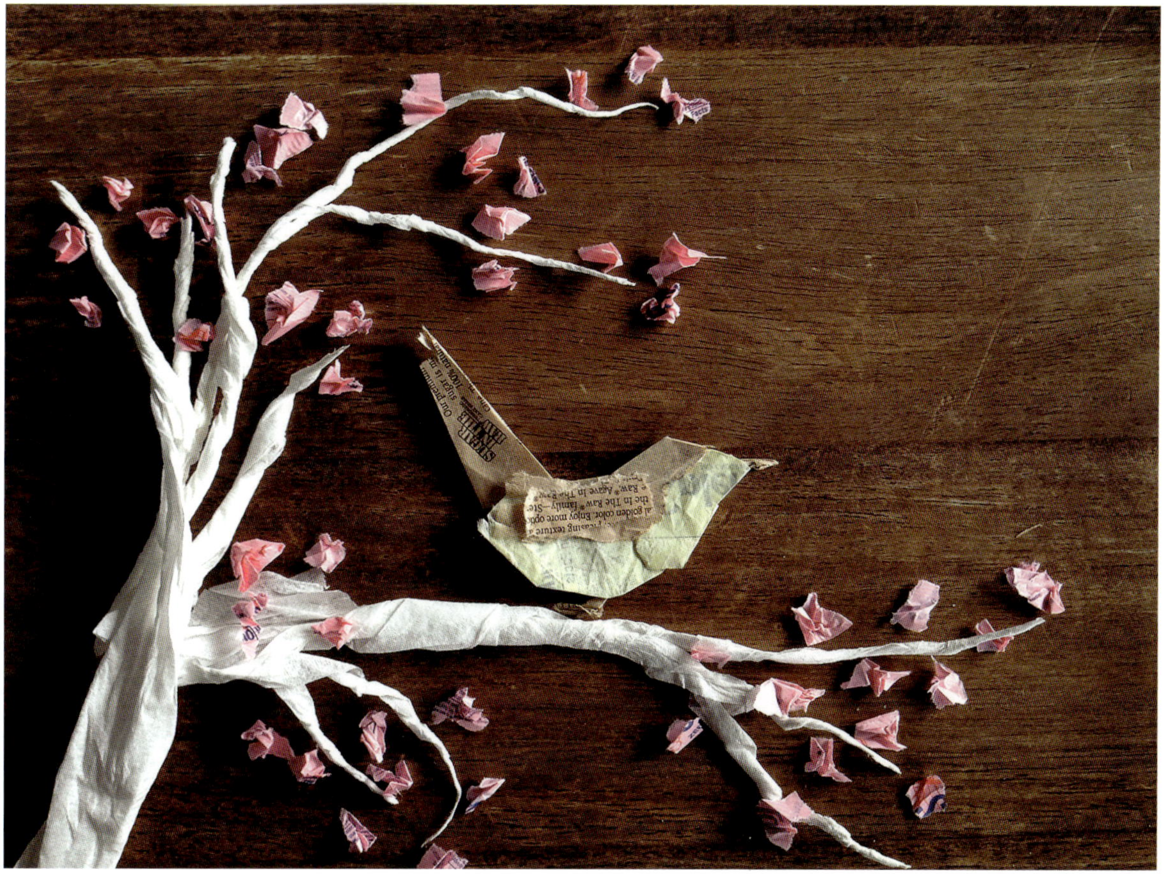

Carolina Wren in the Redbuds
Brian D. Parker, 2014

MOTHER'S DAY

Mom and I were laying on the kitchen floor recovering from a fit of laughter. I had just finished kindergarten and it was a humid day. We were enjoying the cool linoleum, face to face in opposite directions, watching our backward mouths talk. (See diagram A.) I held my hand so all I could see was her mouth and chin. It looked like an eyeless bald man that frowned when Mom laughed. (See diagram B.) She told me about when she and her sister

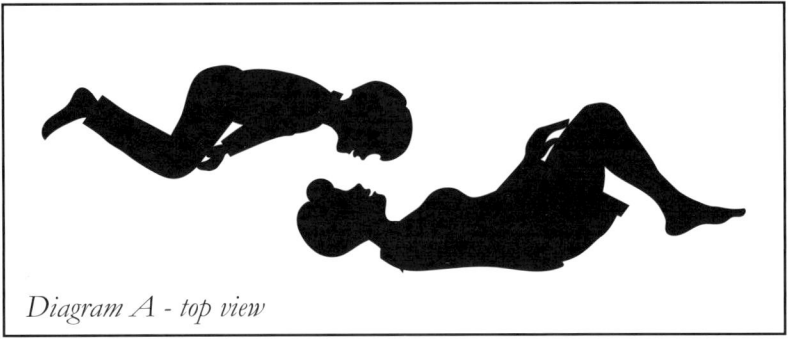

Diagram A - top view

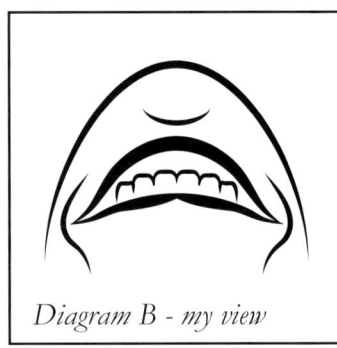

Diagram B - my view

would lie on the floor like this watching each other's mouths. I watched her inverted lips move as she told the story and I started giggling. She laughed and it started it all over again. The harder she laughed, the harder the bald man frowned. My sides hurt, and I still kept laughing. Mom could be serious and in charge, but she knew when and how to laugh.

She taught me many things about life and love. There are a few skills I didn't learn from Mom—although she tried. I didn't learn the habit of cleaning my room, and I didn't learn the habit of balancing my checkbook. But I did learn the habit of silliness. I learned everyday to find joy and a laugh, and I think that is the best skill of all.

Happy Mother's Day, Mom.

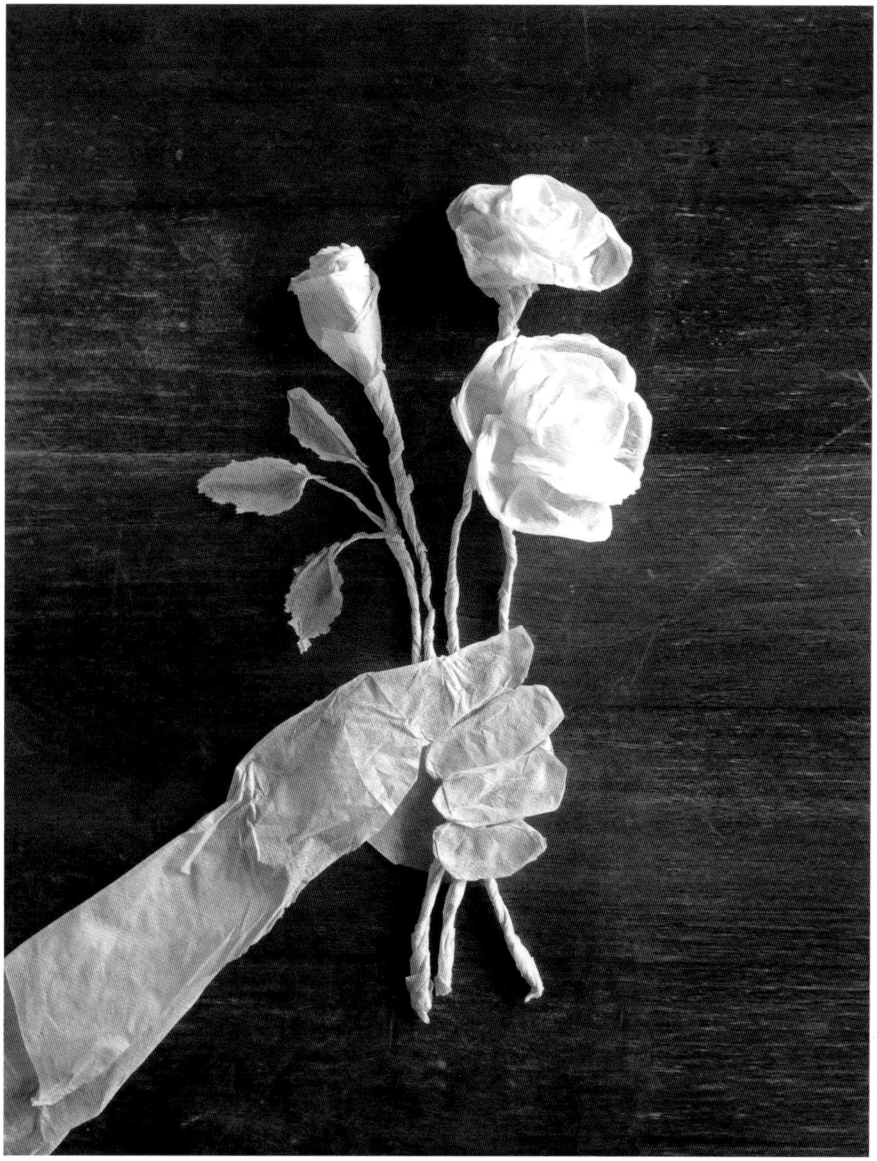

Mother's Day Roses
Brian D. Parker, 2014

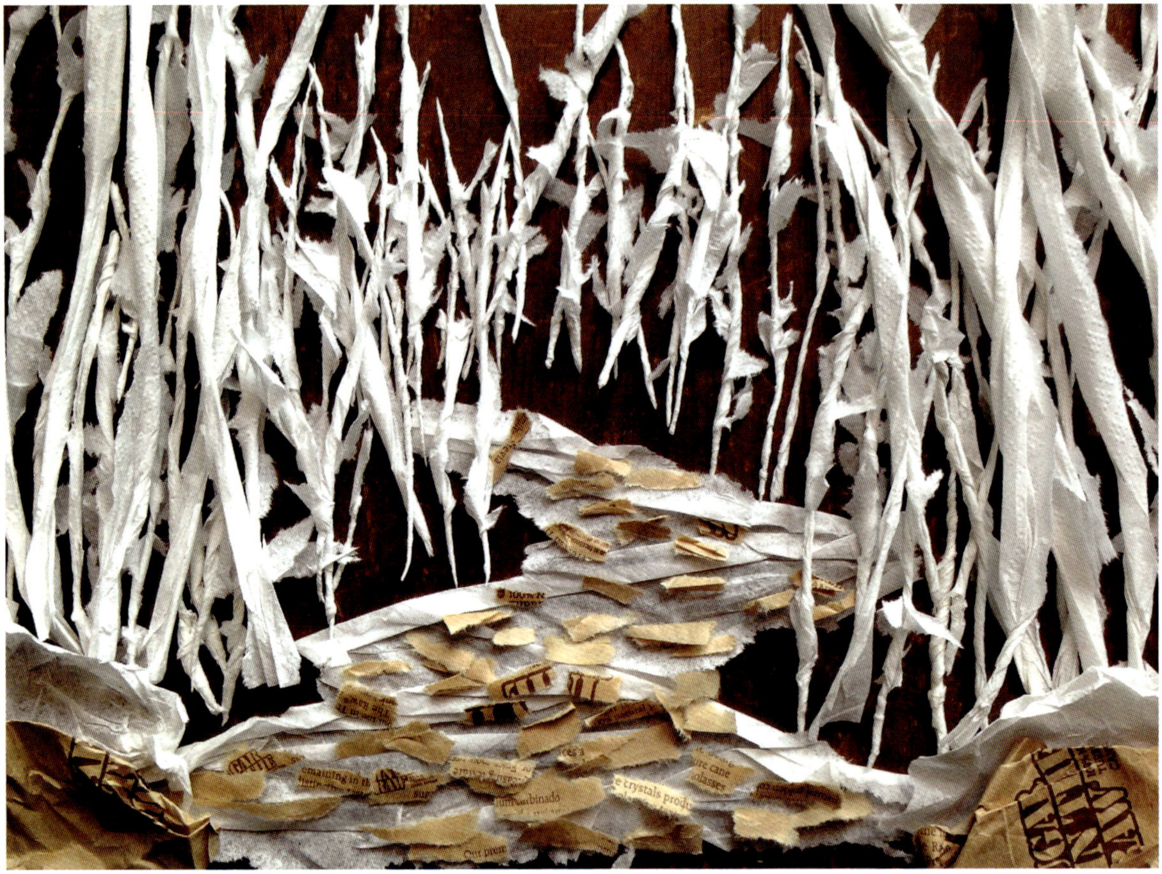

Bamboo Gardens at Cheekwood
Brian D. Parker, 2014

SUMMER

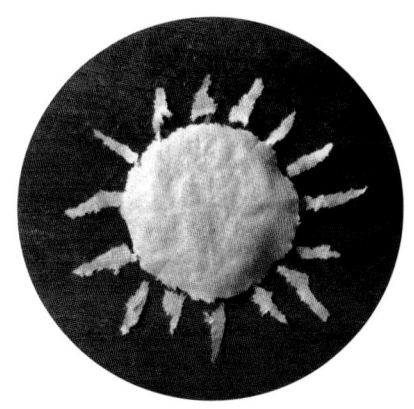

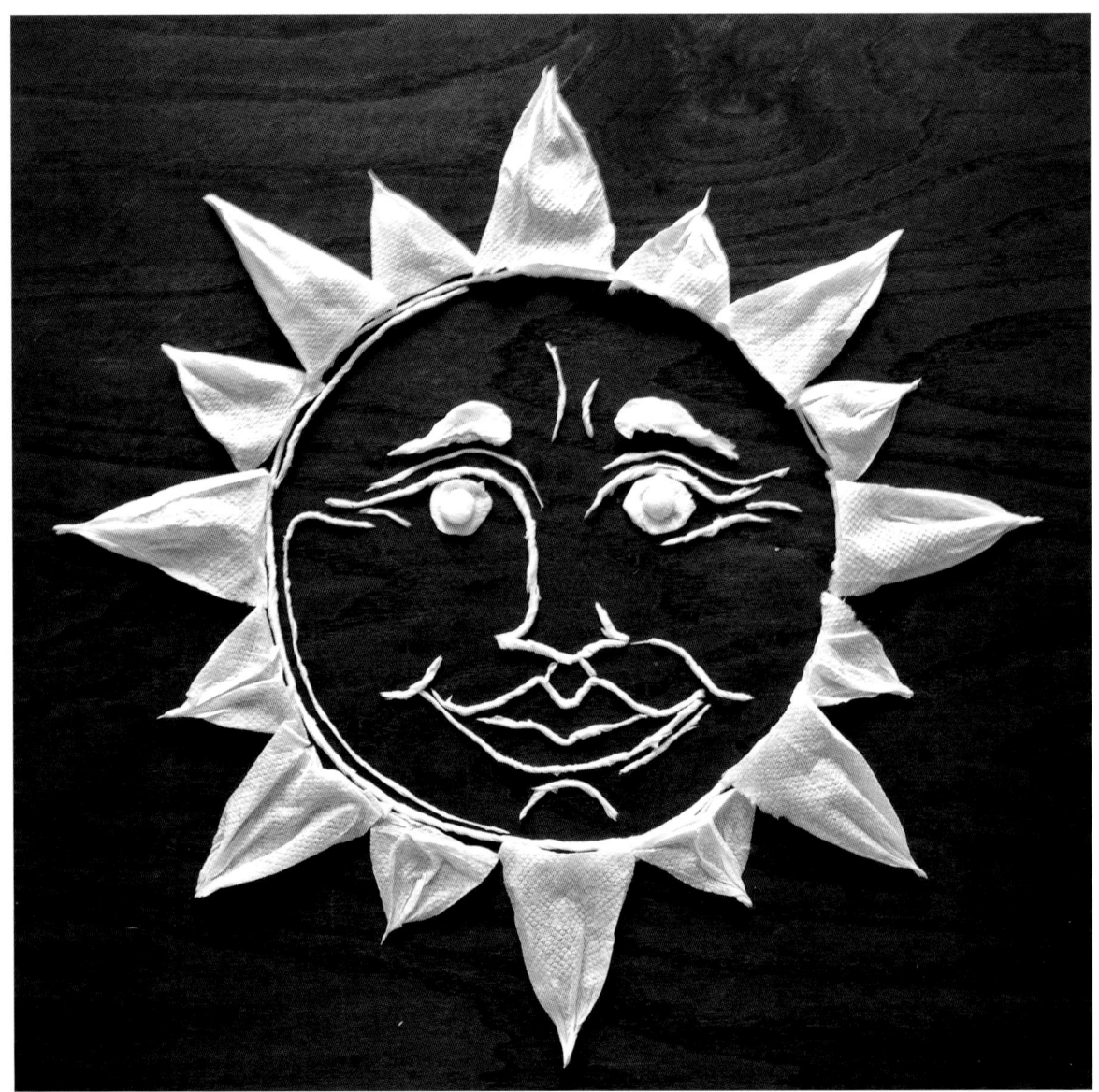

Summer Sun
Brian D. Parker, 2014

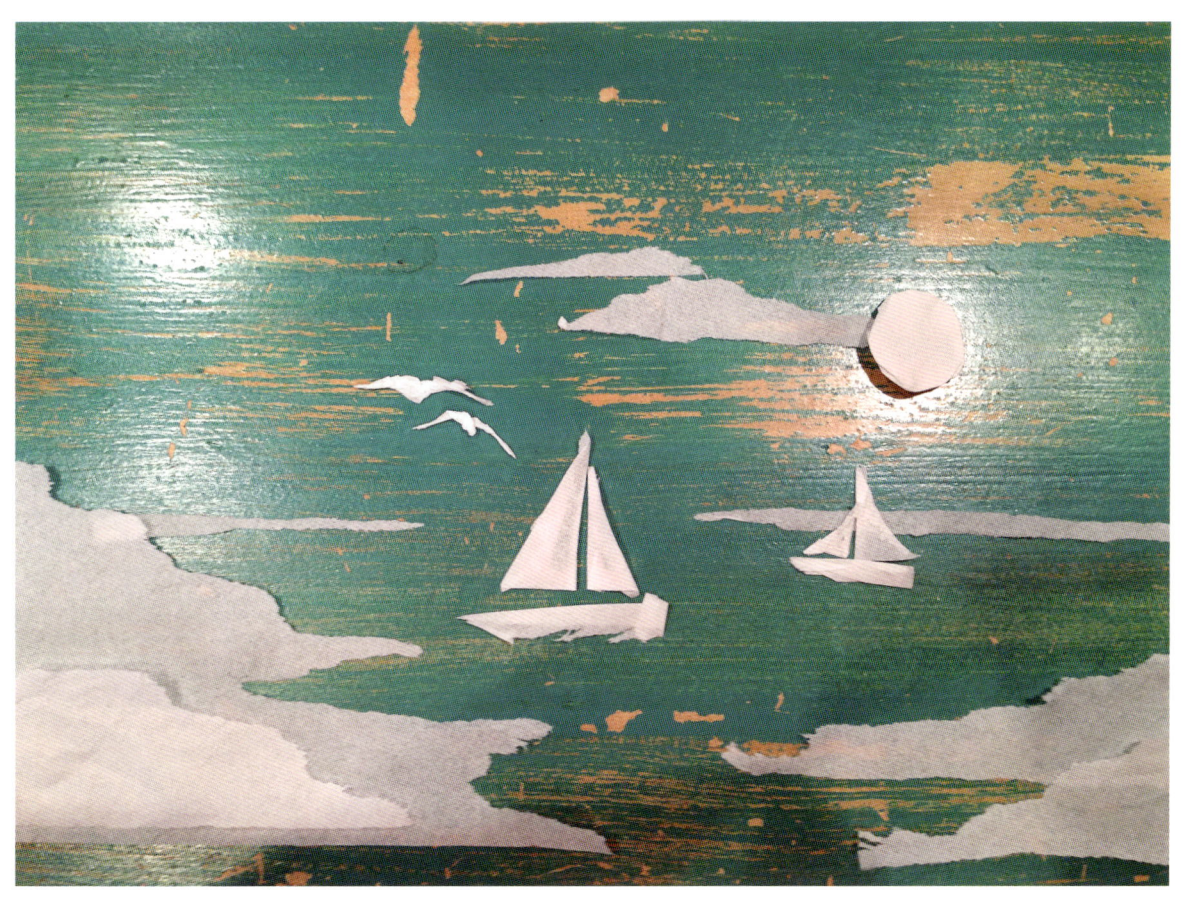

Sailing the Bay
Brian D. Parker, 2014

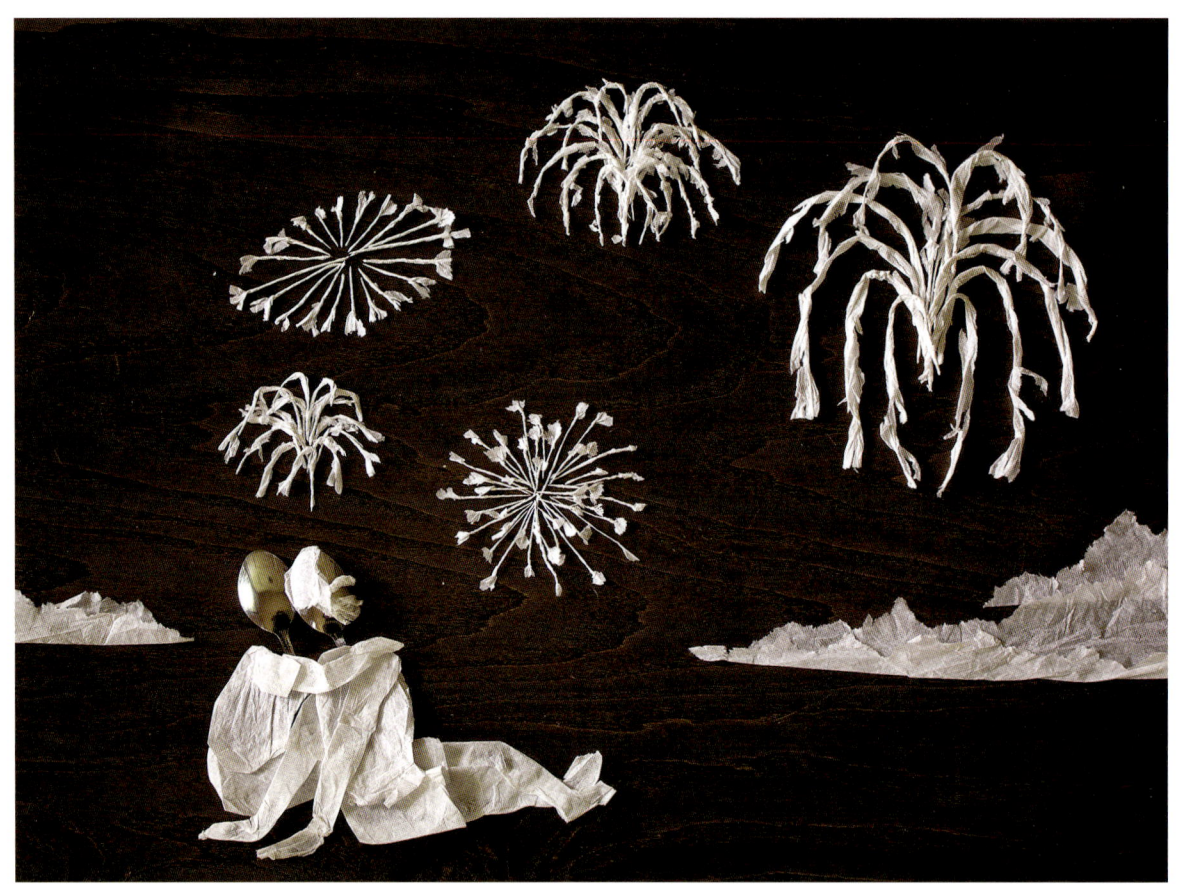

Fireworks from East Park
Brian D. Parker, 2014

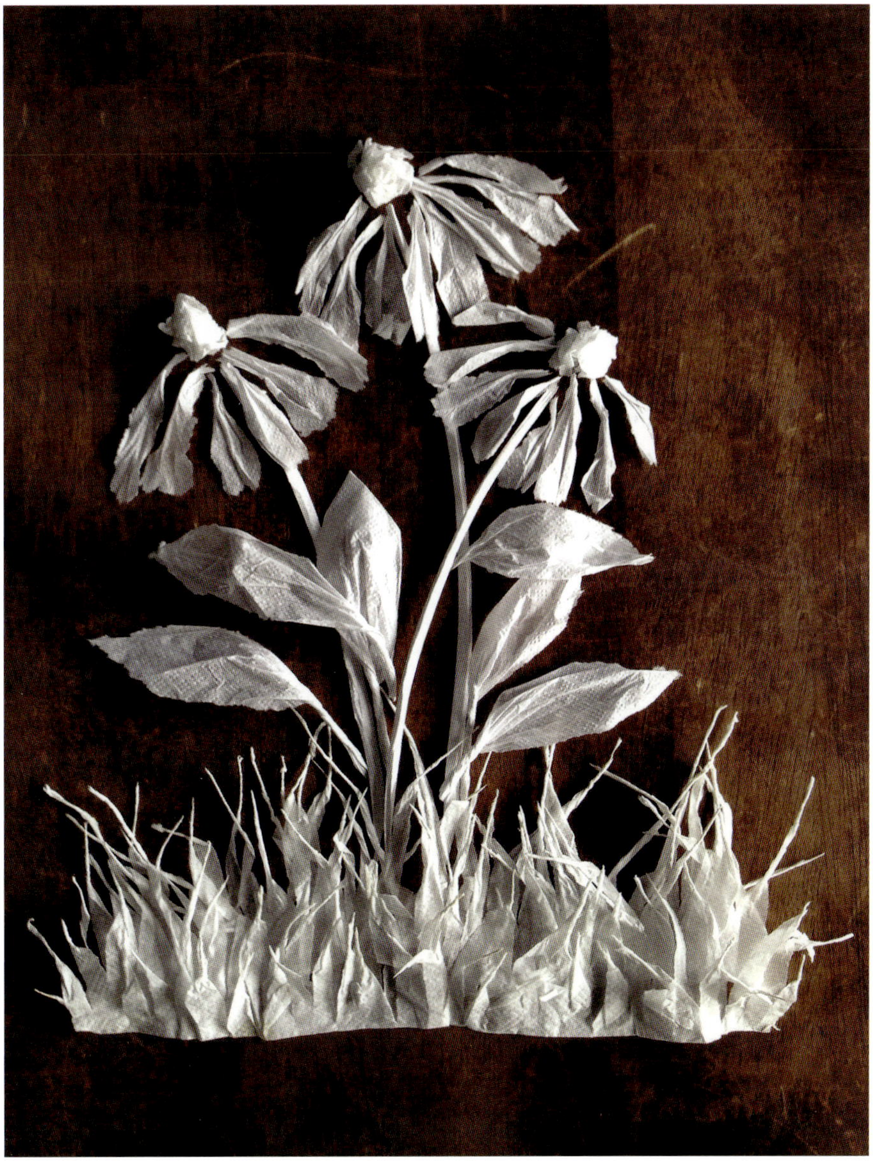

Coneflowers
Brian D. Parker, 2014

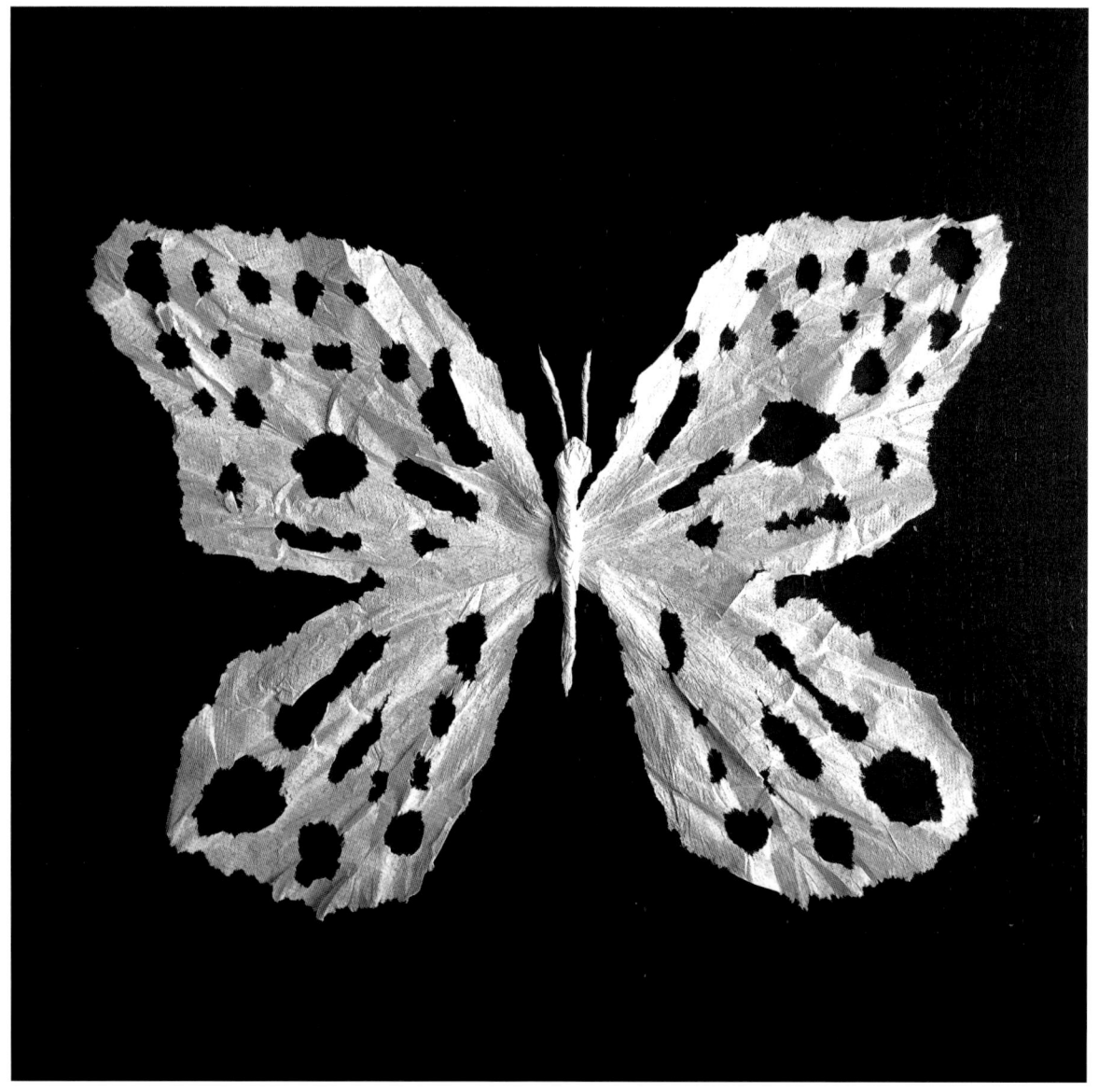

Butterfly 1
Brian D. Parker, 2014

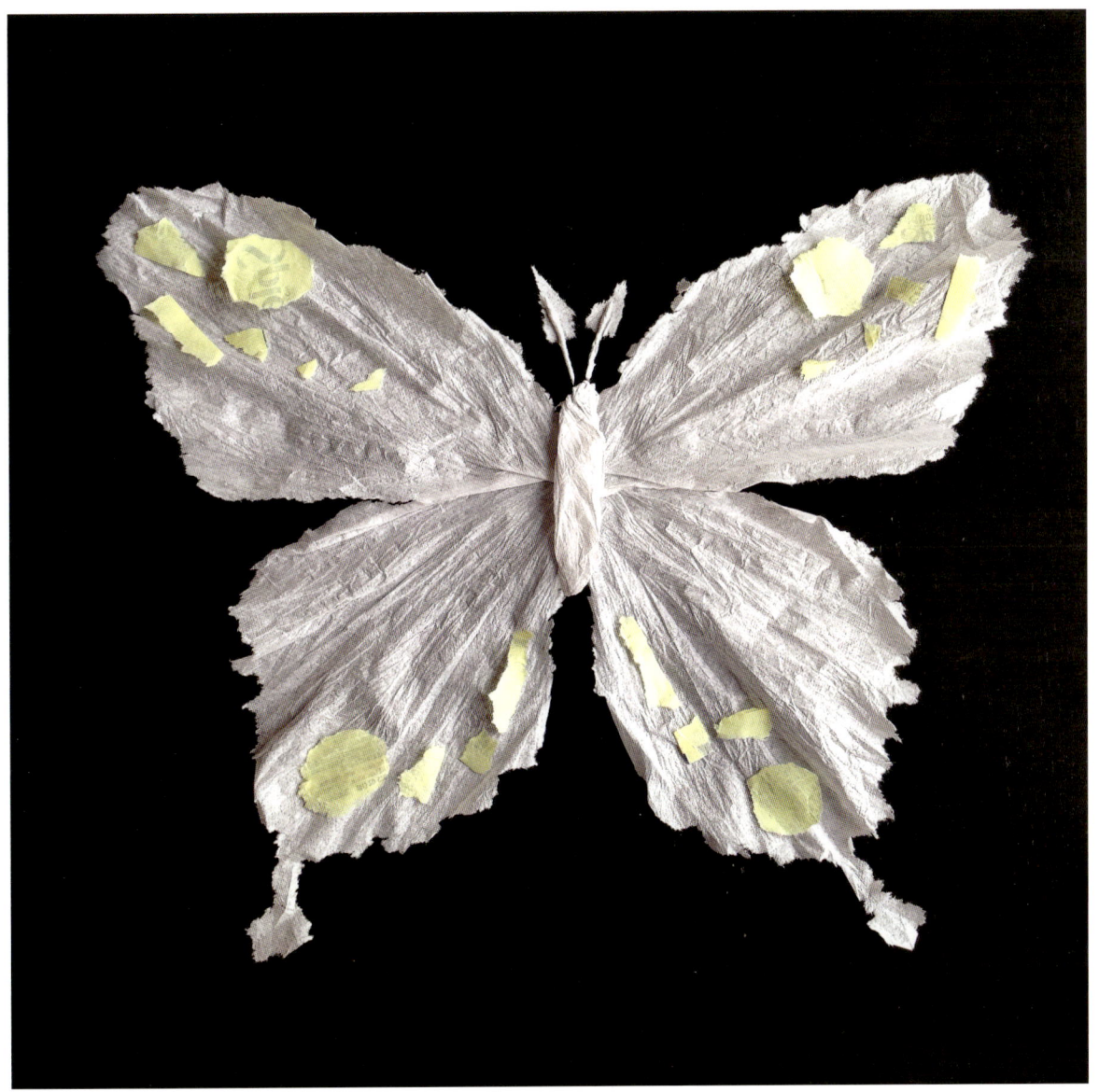

Butterfly 2
Brian D. Parker, 2014

FATHER'S DAY

Dad is many things—husband, father, grandfather. Add to that: scientist, artist, non-conformist, builder—a Renaissance man. But when he's alone with his thoughts, I suspect he's a fly fisherman. I hesitate to put such a specific label on Dad, but I remember once how his face lit up with romance when he talked about fly fishing in Montana. He always seemed dreamy-eyed when he spoke of the Big Sky Country.

Dad taught me how to tie flies when I was kid. I remember my first look inside the special box. It was full of hooks, hackle, spools of colored chenille, and exotic iridescent feathers. Dad pulled out the tools and materials and began to demonstrate. I learned how to trim and bend feathers into a tiny loops that looked like insect wings. I stripped and bent quills into grasshopper legs. It was a satisfying new form of sculpture, made more satisfying because it pleased Dad.

He didn't have a lot of time to himself. All of his roles kept him busy with work, family, and church. Dad seemed happy to fill those roles, but I know, at times, he wished for the solitude of fishing a quiet river.

Years ago, Robert Redford made the movie *A River Runs Through It.* If Dad had been a fly-fishing obsessed Presbyterian minister and my brother had been murdered over gambling debt, it could have been my story. It could have been a great tragedy to tell strangers at bars. People would buy me drinks and shake their heads with sympathy. I confess I love a tragedy. But for all it's boring "Cleaver-ness," I'm glad Dad and I have had a mostly drama-free relationship. He is a man full of endurance, wisdom, ingenuity and, best of all, immoveable, unfailing love. And I am a lucky kid.

Happy Father's Day, Dad.

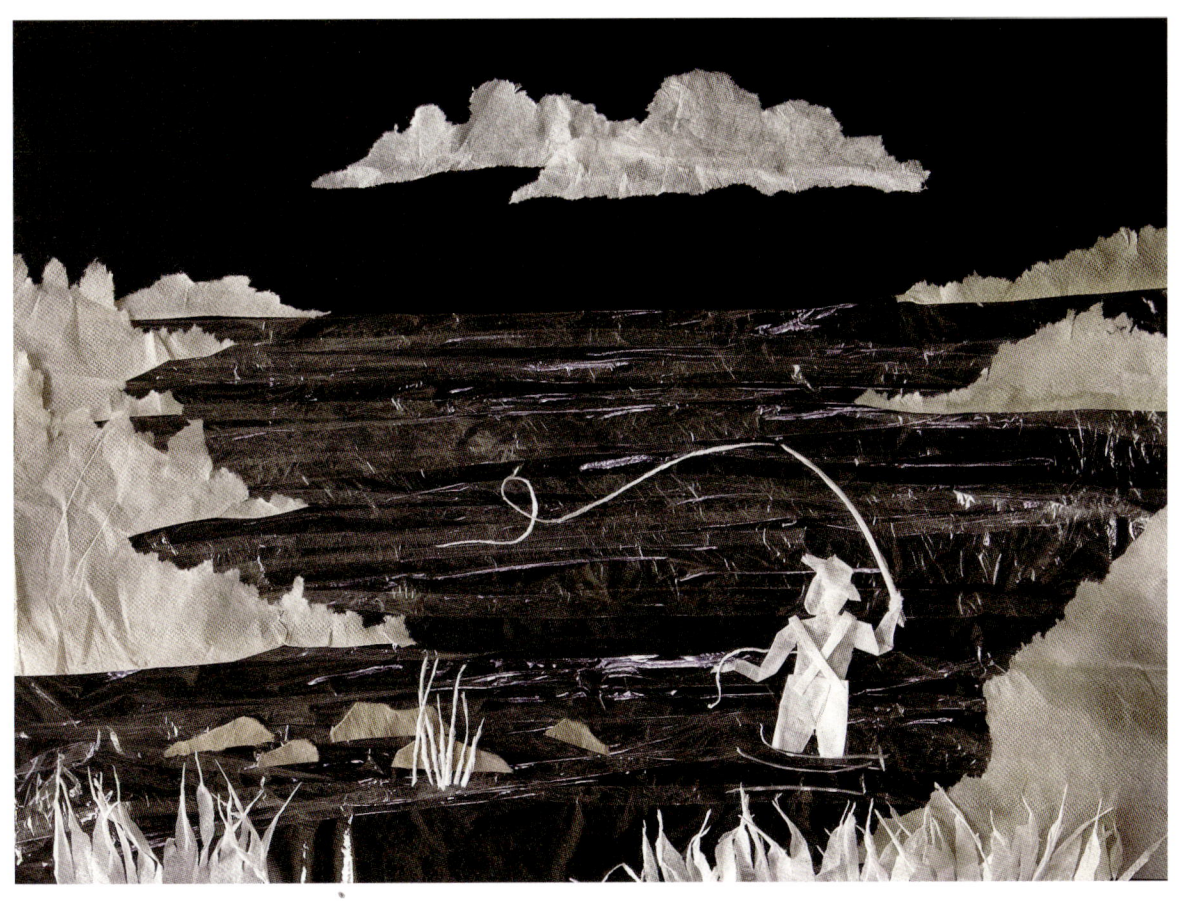

Forward Cast
Brian D. Parker, 2014

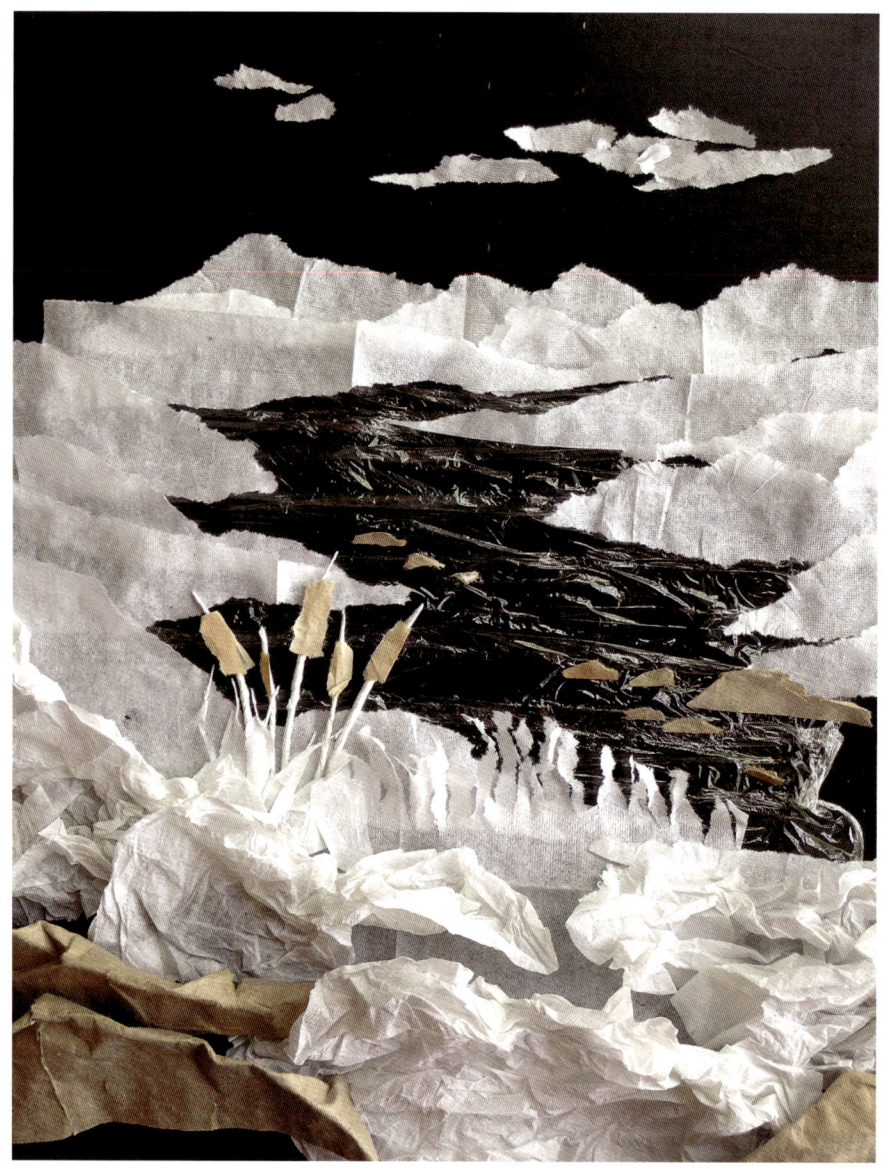

Stones River
Brian D. Parker, 2014

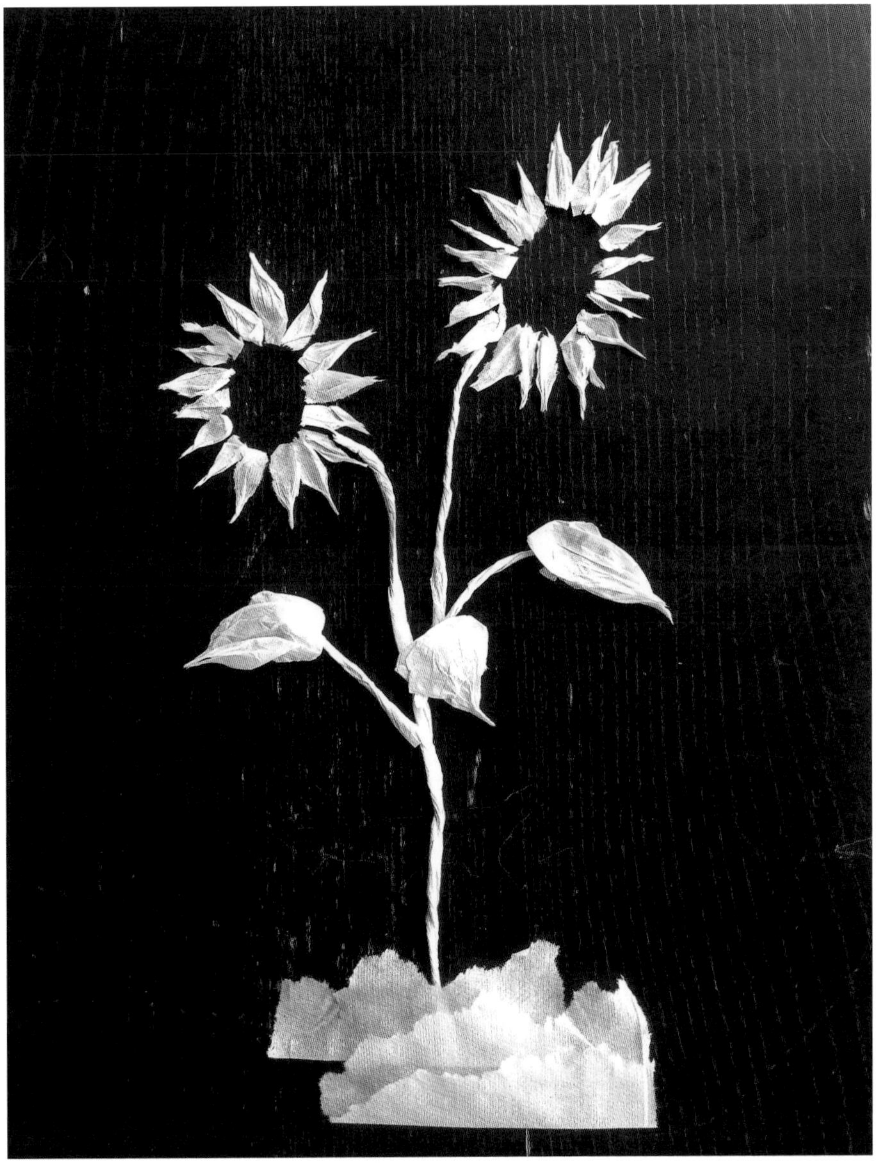

Sunflowers
Brian D. Parker, 2014

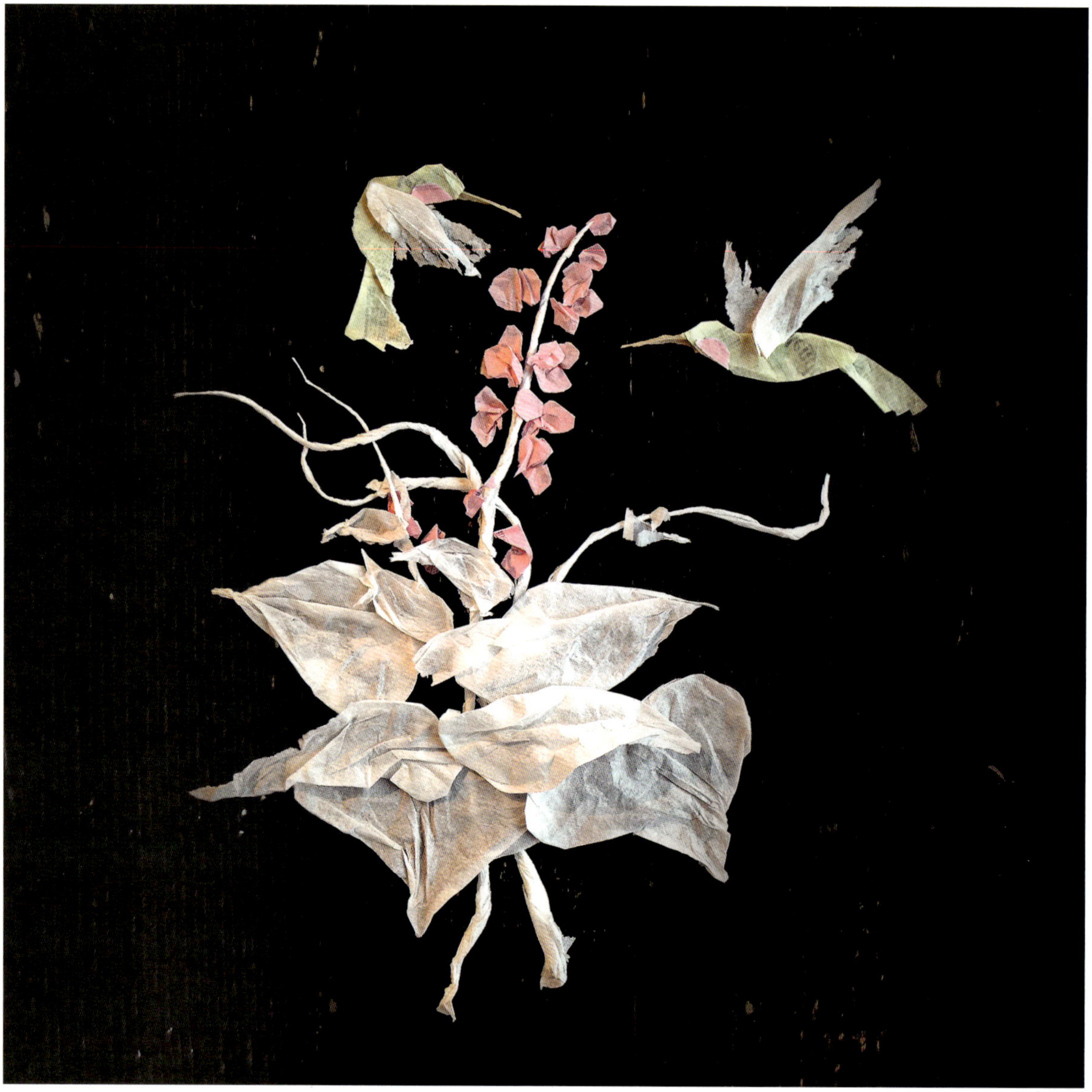

Hummingbirds in the Hyacinth Bean
Brian D. Parker, 2014

AUTUMN

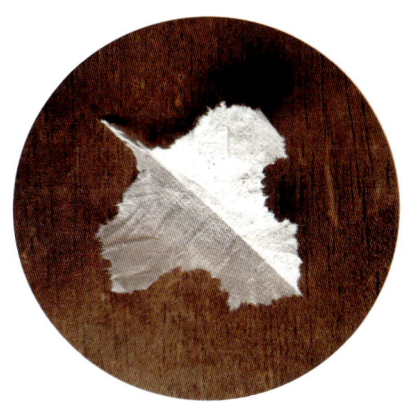

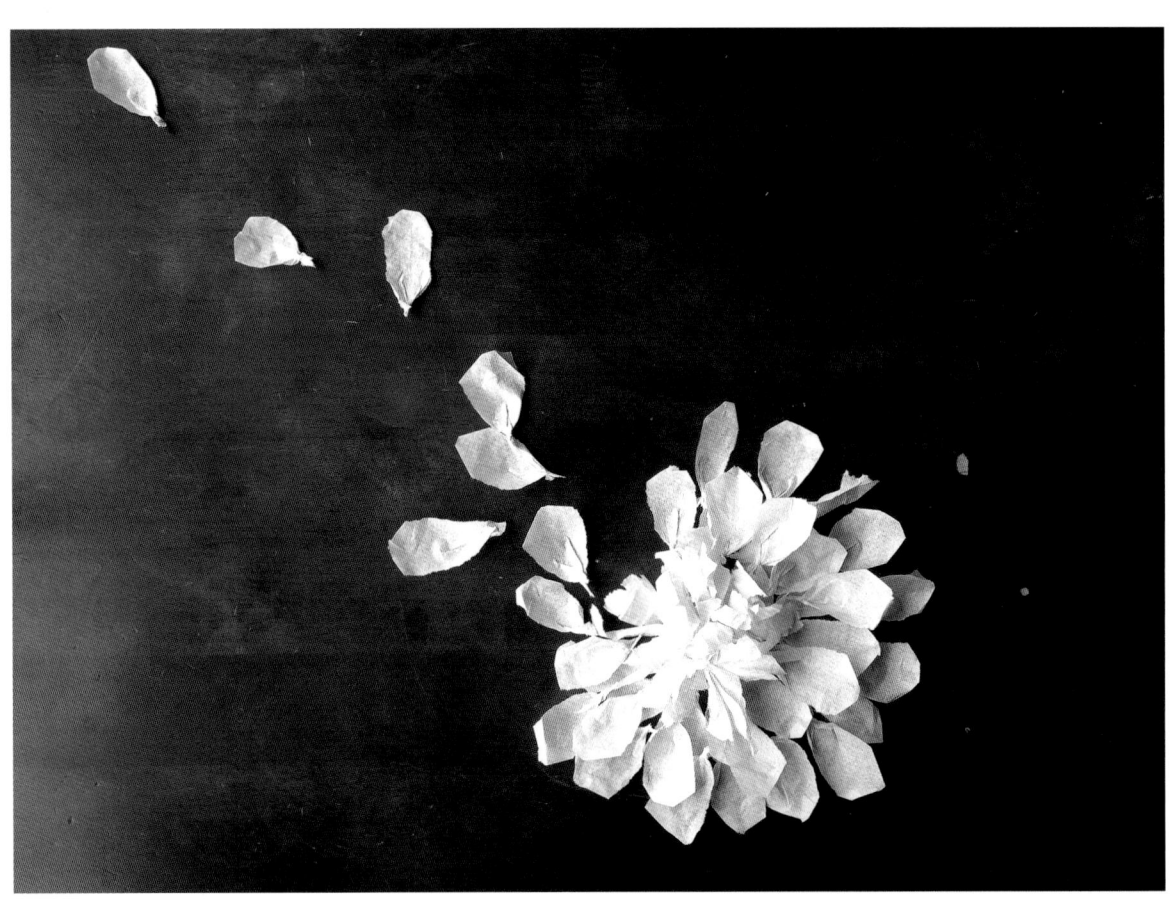

Blowing Flower
Brian D. Parker, 2014

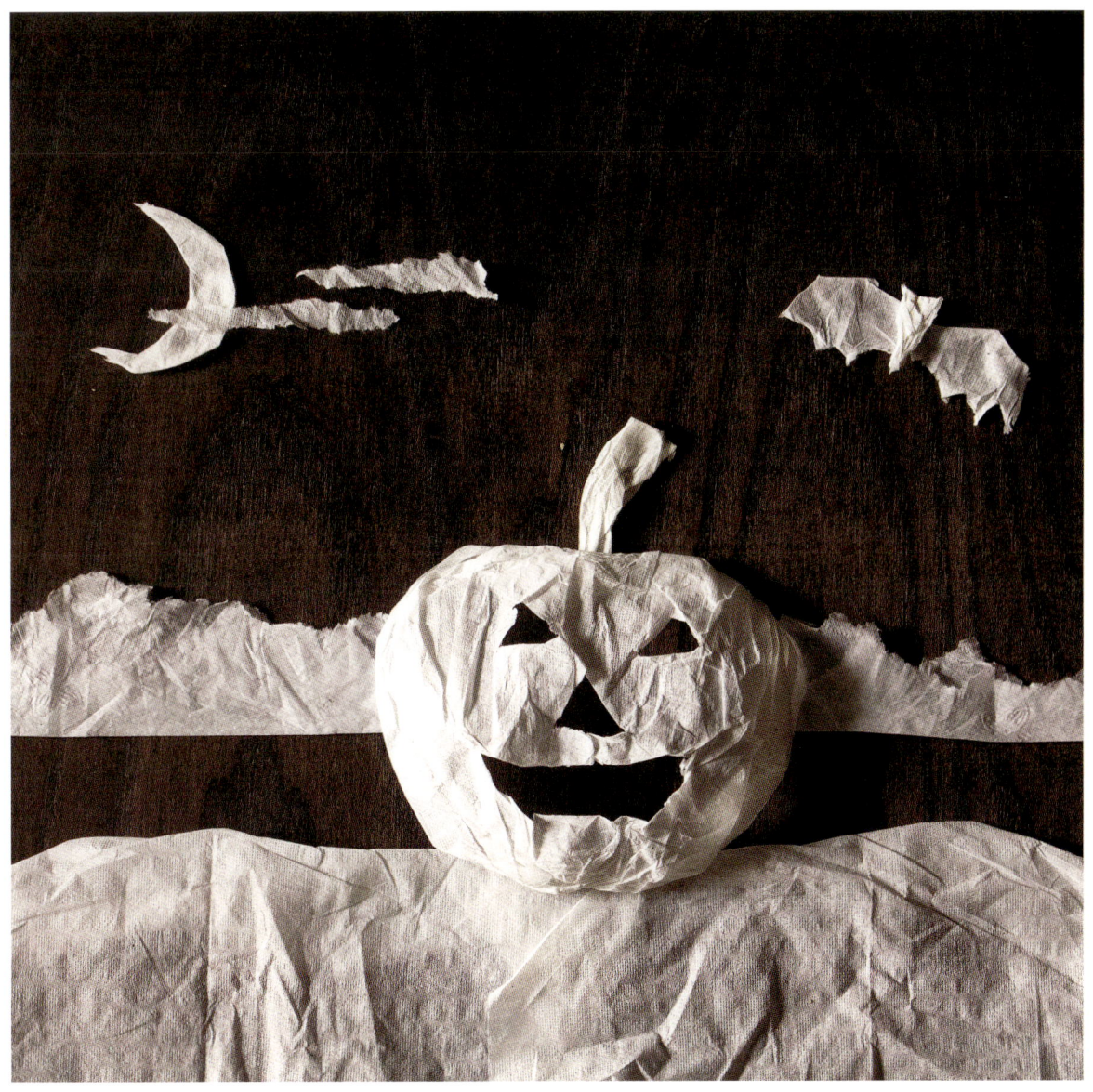

Jack-o-lantern
Brian D. Parker, 2014

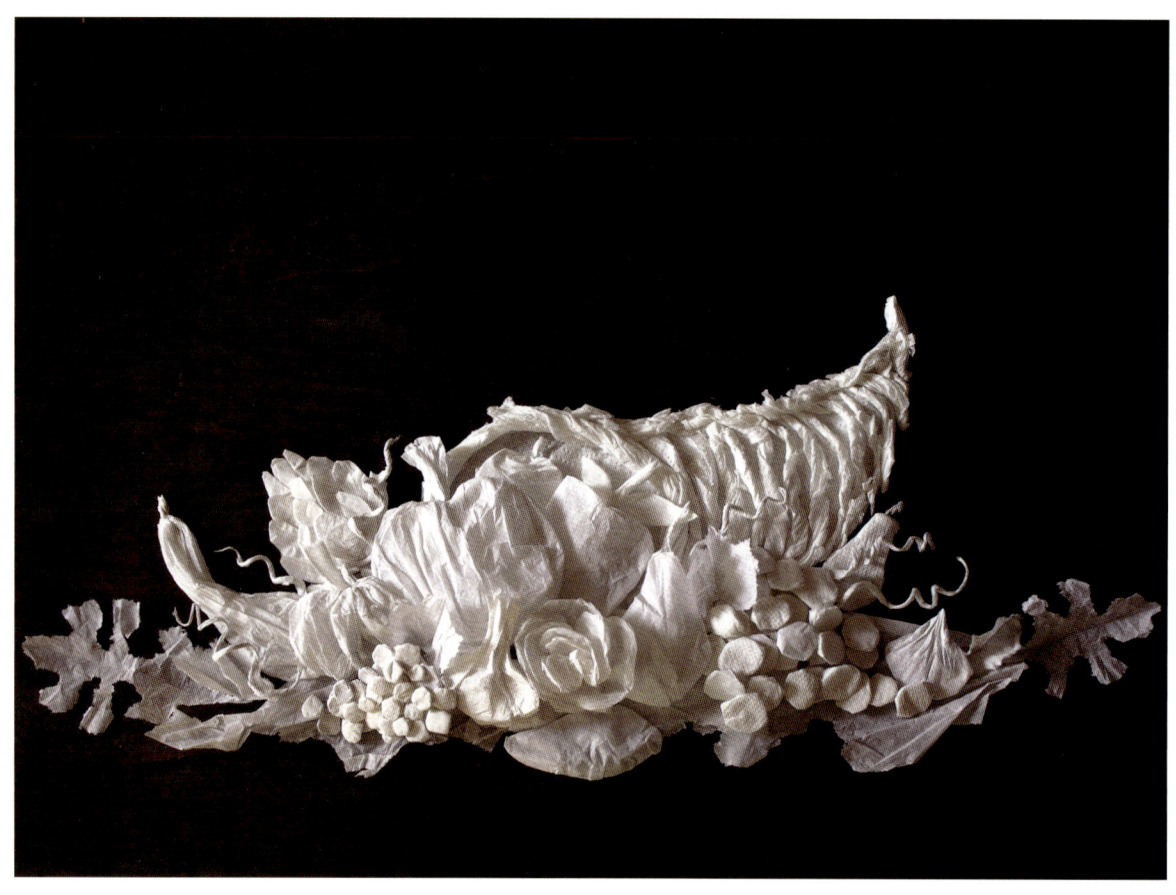

Cornucopia
Brian D. Parker, 2014

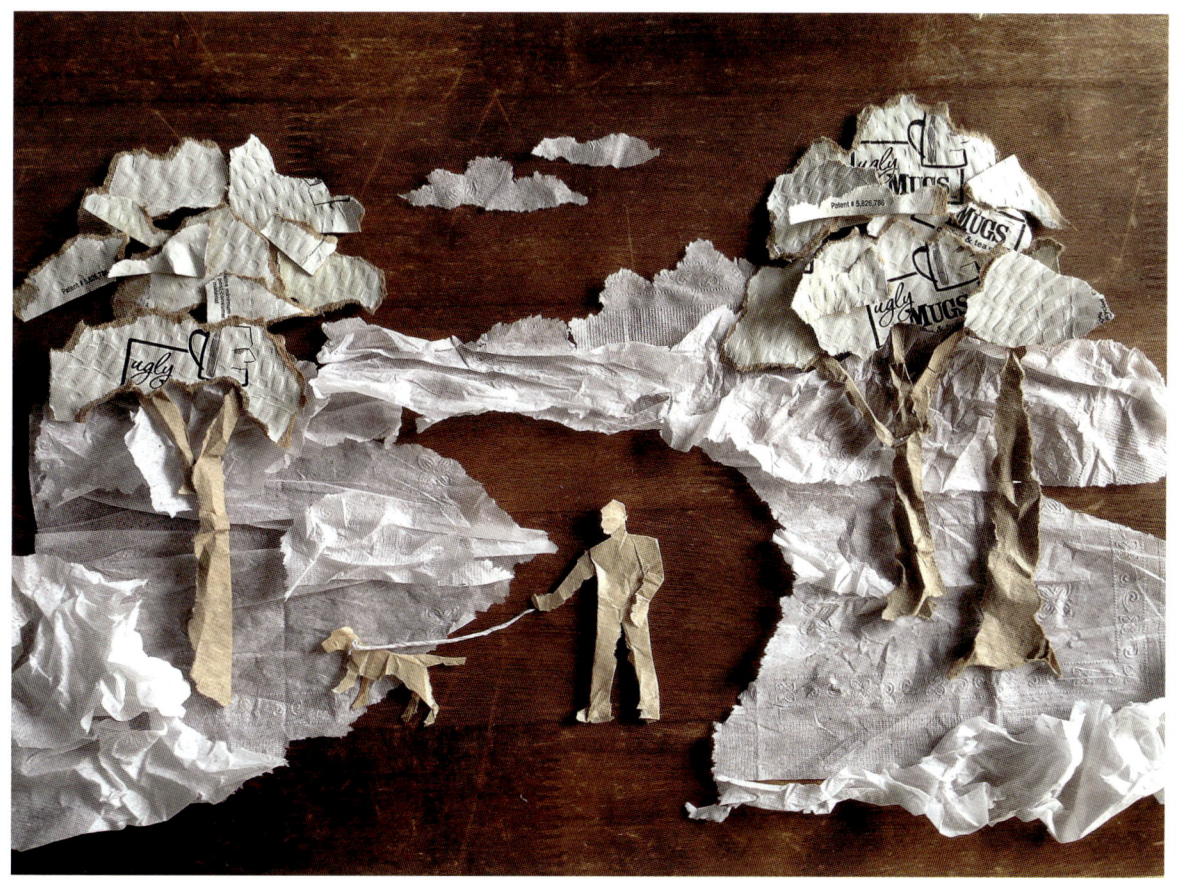

Gussy and Me
Brian D. Parker, 2014

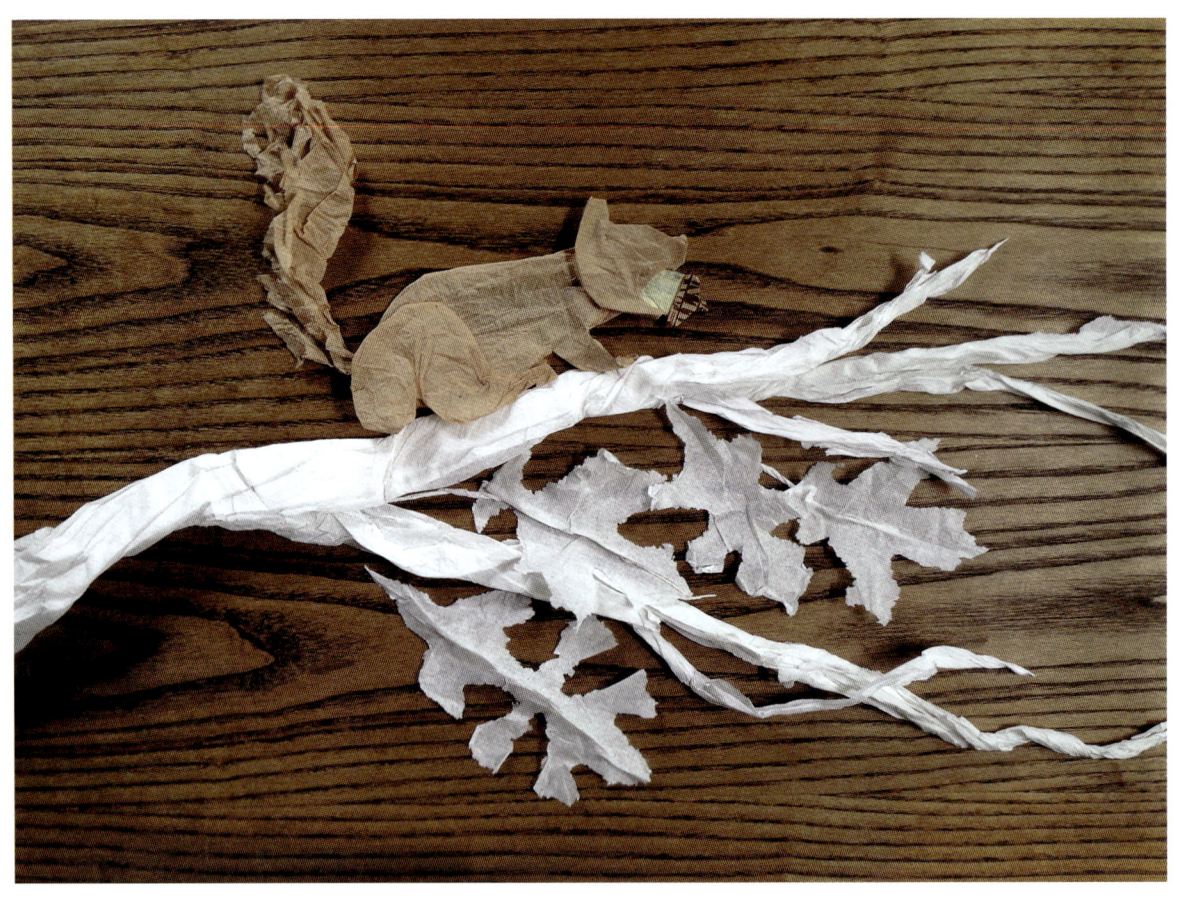

Squirreling for Winter
Brian D. Parker, 2014

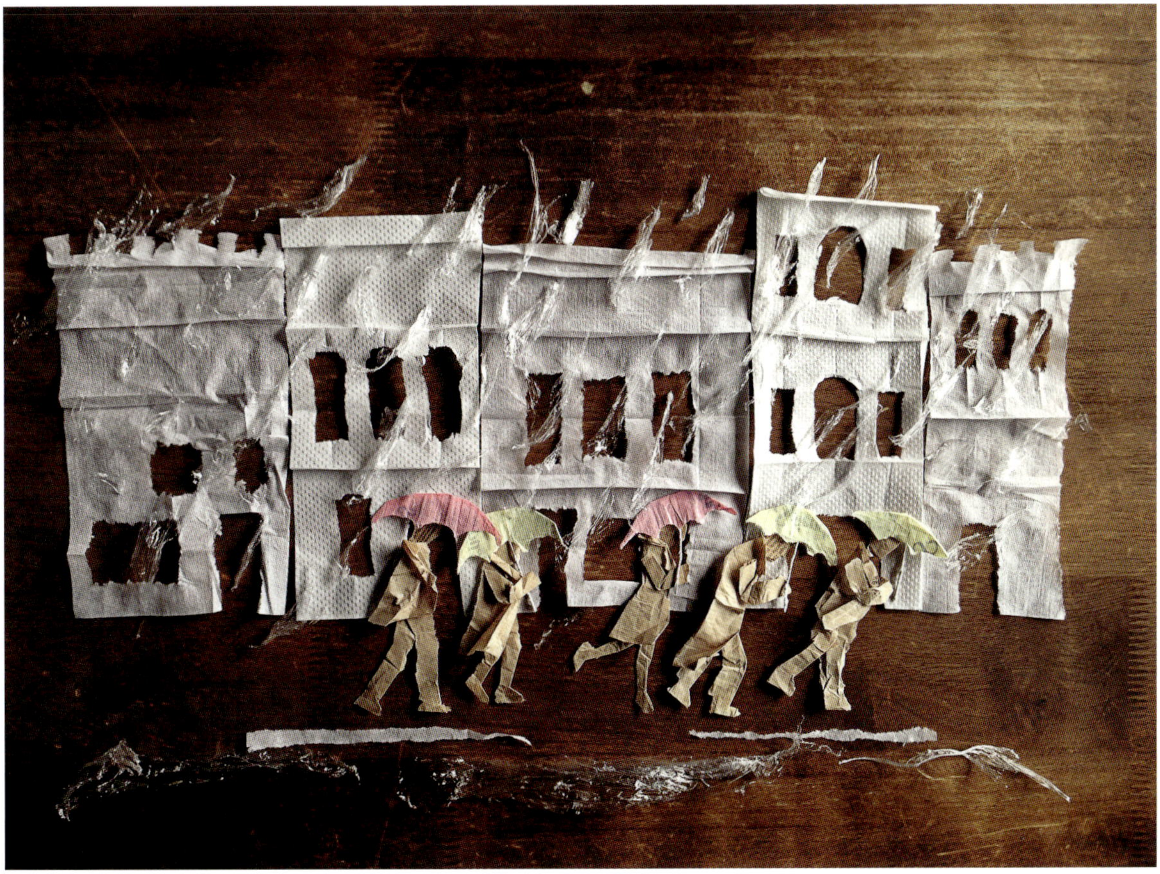

Rainy Day on Second Ave
Brian D. Parker, 2014

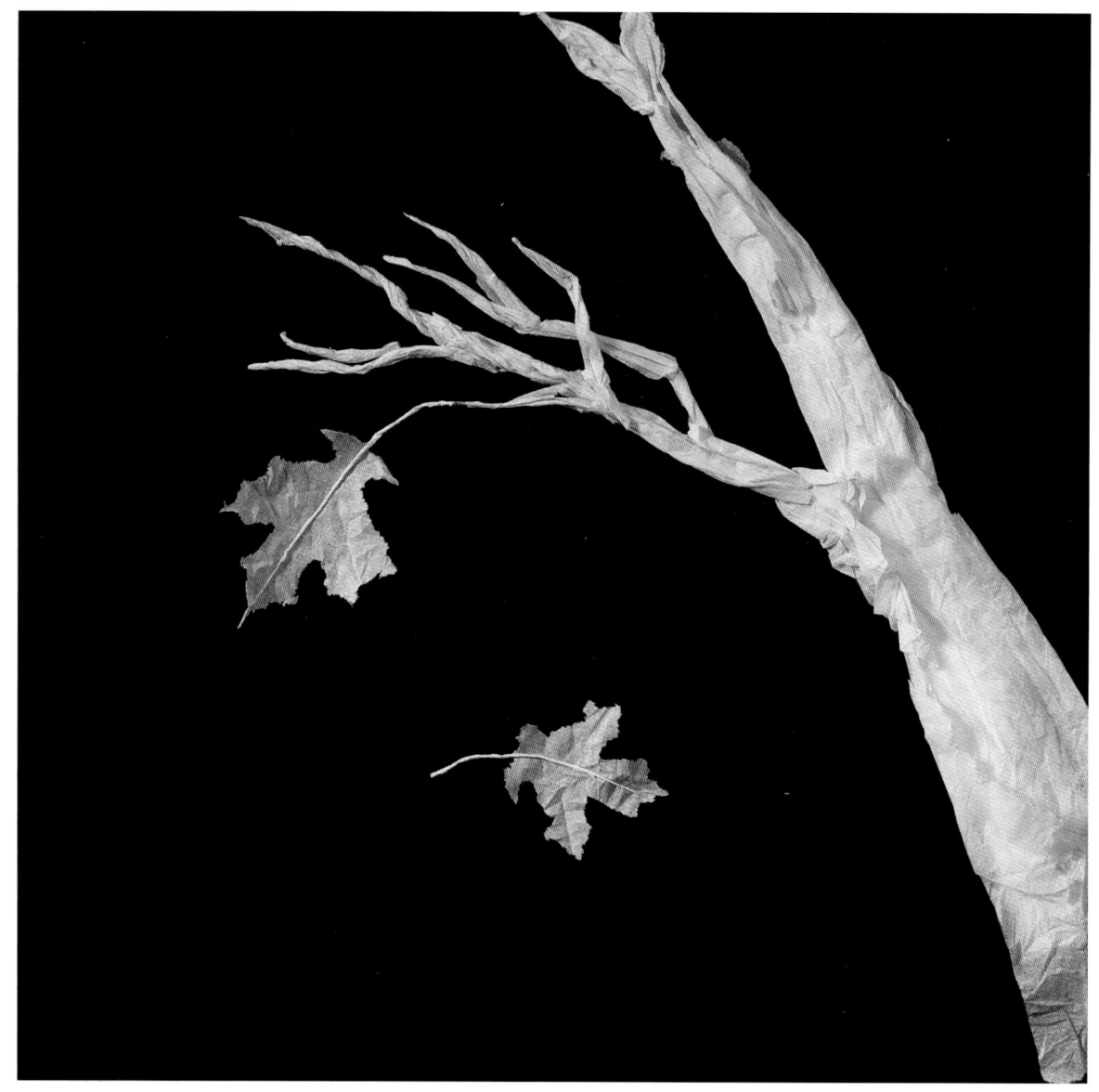

Falling Leaves
Brian D. Parker, 2014

WINTER

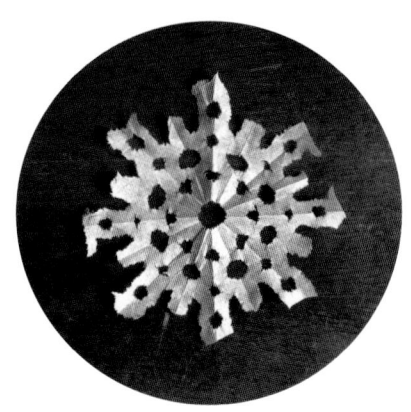

HELGESON PARK

I was shocked when Jim told me it was named Helgeson Park. He said, "Go look at the sign for yourself if you don't believe me." There was a sign? I wondered how in all of my eight years I could have missed a "Helgeson Park" sign? The thought bothered me. It was surreal, like discovering a shocking secret about a friend, or when I found out Mom had a name—Carol Parker. That was still weird. I wasn't sure I could make the shift. The park had a name, and it wasn't Helgeson Park. It was Poop Hill.

It was called Poop Hill because it was close to the sewage plant. I had never thought twice about the name. It was just a really fun place. This old park, an old friend, was more than just a sign. Special things happened there, and the real magic happened in winter.

On December evenings, the whole neighborhood gathered for sledding. Onlookers brought lawn chairs and sat with their thermos bottles at the top of the hill. It was like a block party. Some nights were so crowded you had to wait in line for the main run. If you didn't stay on the main run, you risked hitting a pole or picnic table.

We had recently switched from rail sleds to the plastic sheet type. I was glad for the change. The old sleds embarrassed me. They were rusty and reminded me of black and white movies. Some of the rich kids had sleek plastic boat-like sleds and I was jealous, but ours were faster, and on Poop Hill speed was everything. We raced friends and strangers, but almost nothing could beat our "blue blazers." I liked aiming for the dip about halfway down and to the left. If the snow was just right and your sled was waxed, you could catch air.

I wanted those nights to last forever. We would beg for more and Dad would let us go "just one more time." It usually turned into three more times. When we got home, Mom made us Swiss Miss hot chocolate with milk instead of water "to add richness."

No, I could never think of it as Helgeson Park. I went to find the sign for myself, and it was there—a small granite monument with the words, "Helgeson Memorial Park." But it didn't matter. I wasn't going to use this just-discovered name. Everything I knew, I knew. And a sign wouldn't change that. My fondness *and* the name were already solidified in the pure crystal drifts of Poop Hill.

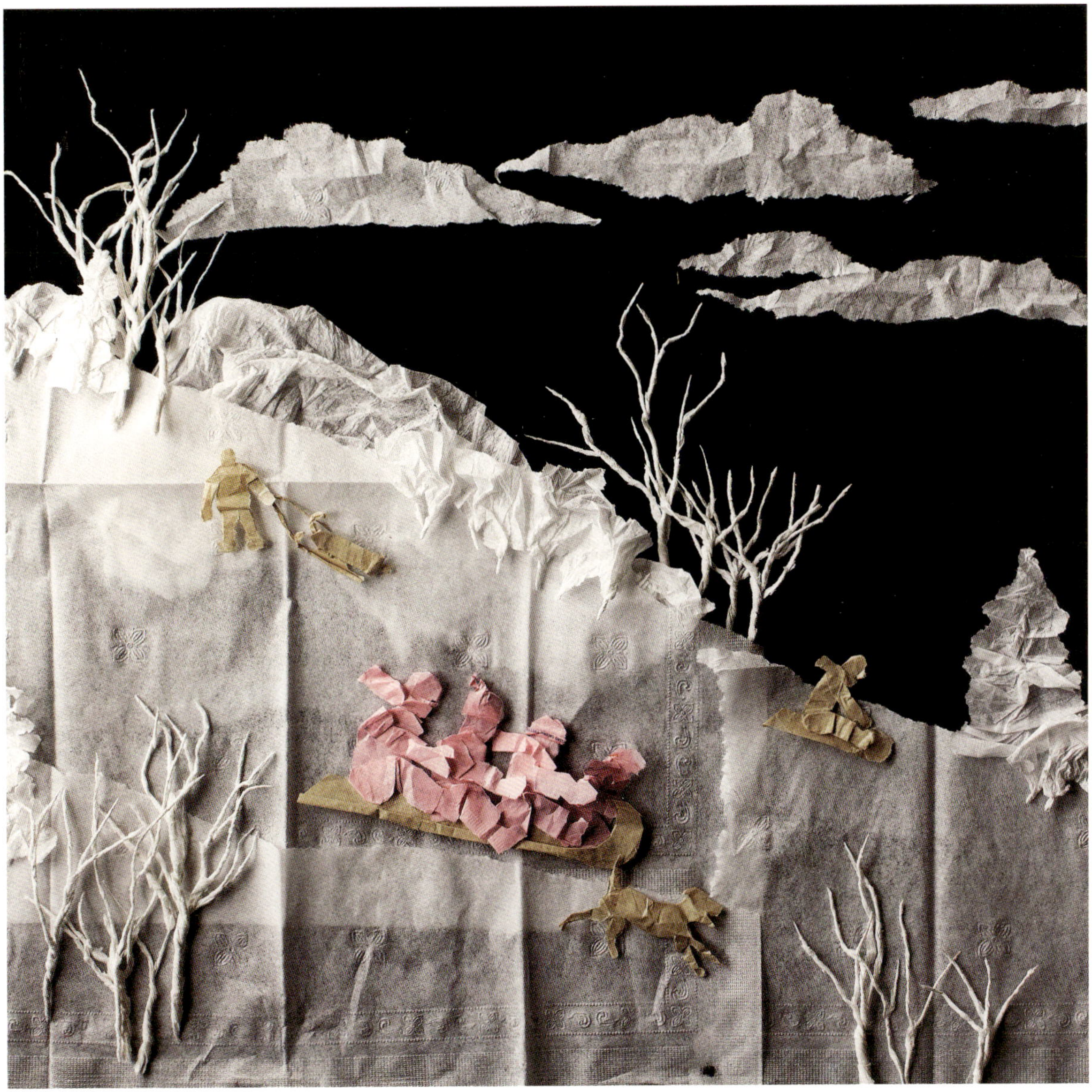

Helgeson Park
Brian D. Parker, 2014

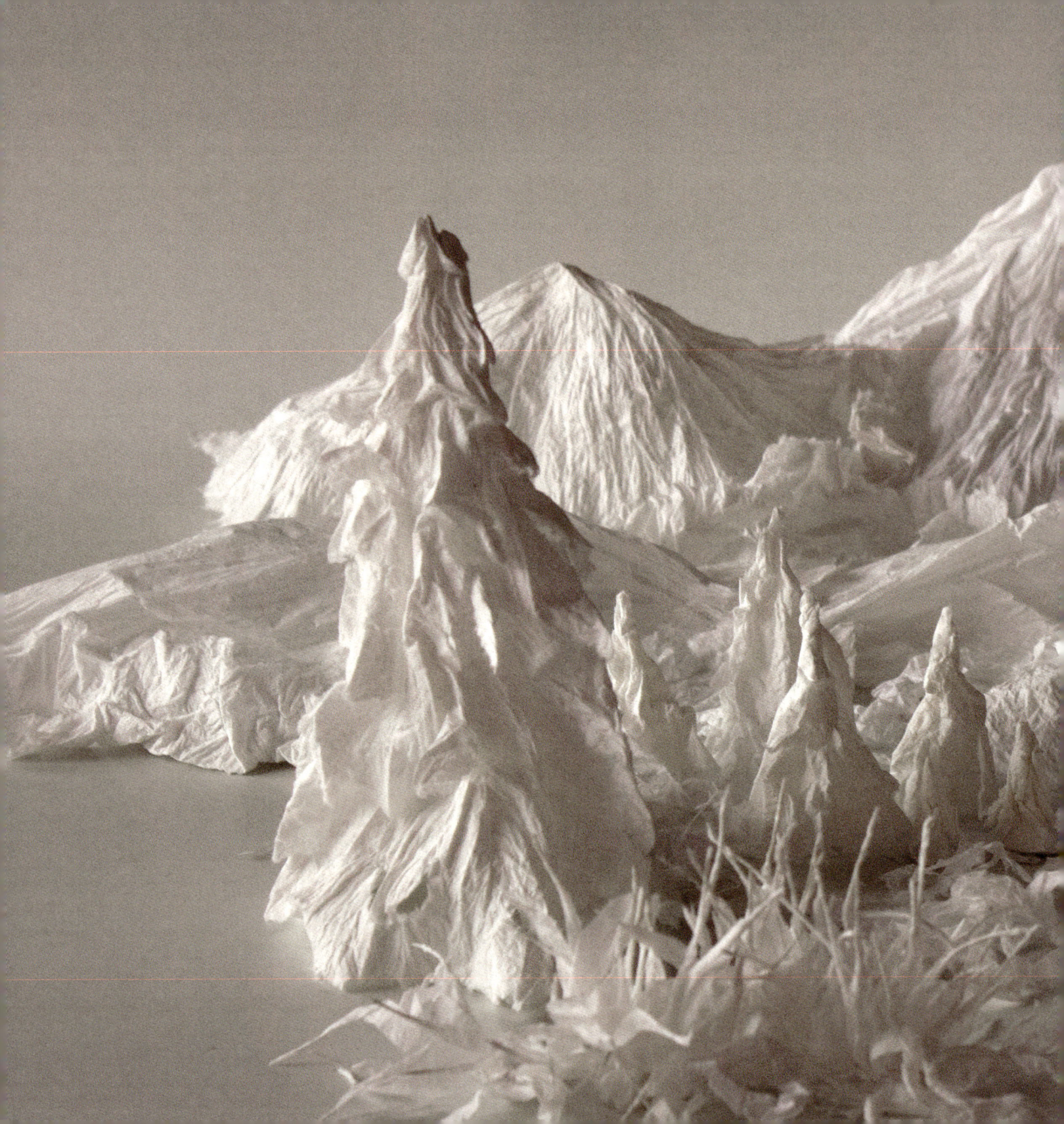

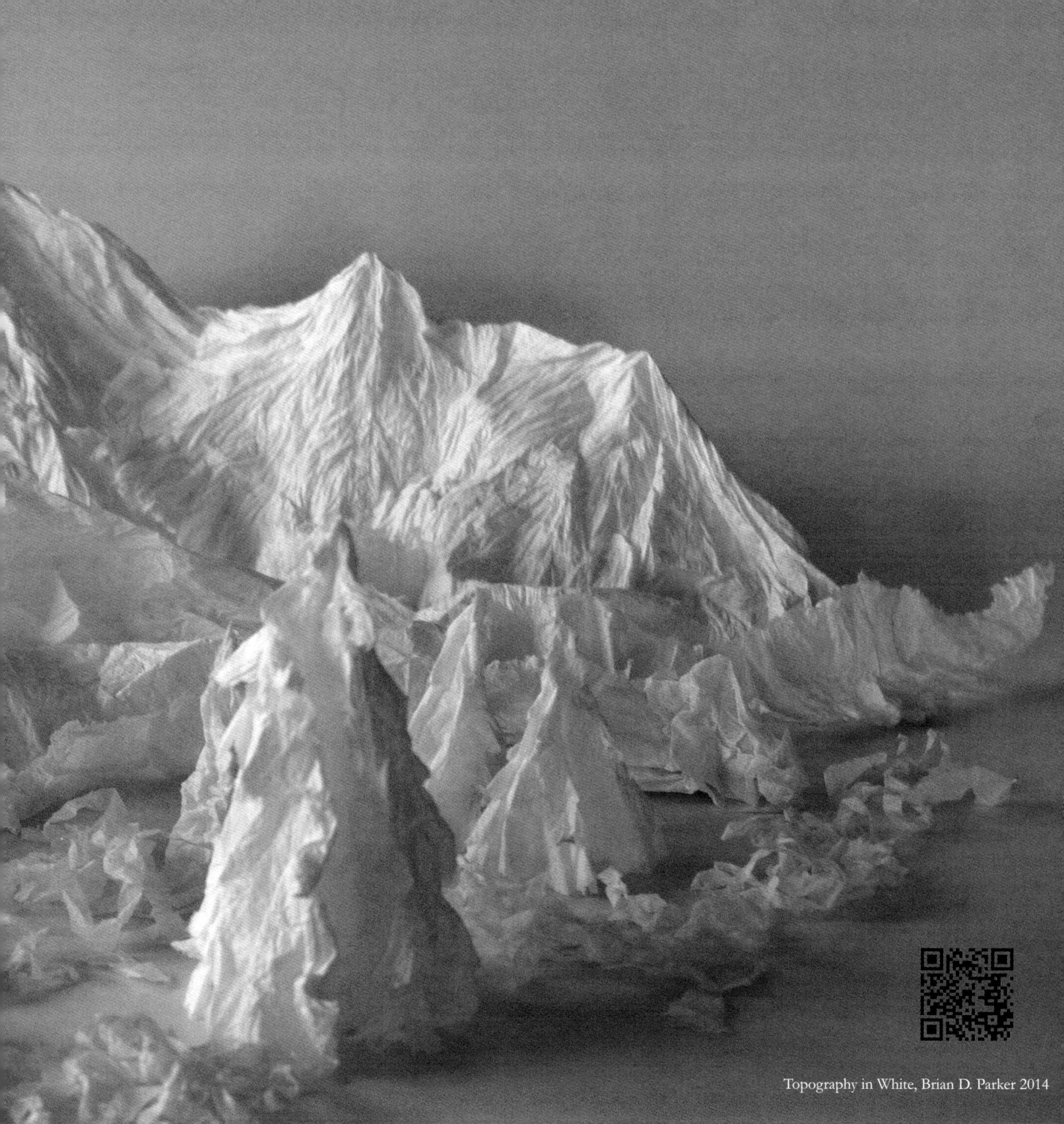

Topography in White, Brian D. Parker 2014

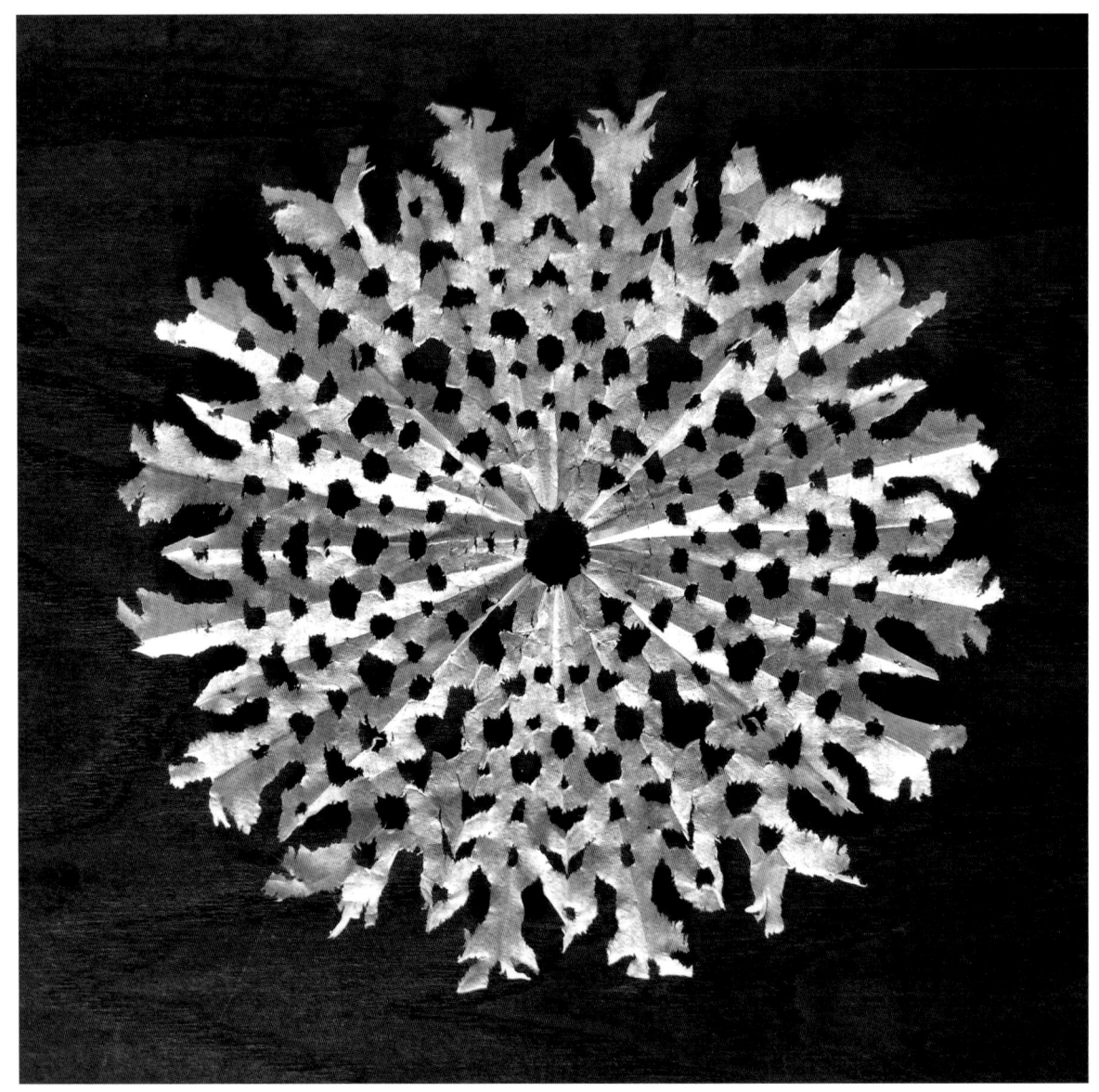

Snowflake 1
Brian D. Parker, 2014

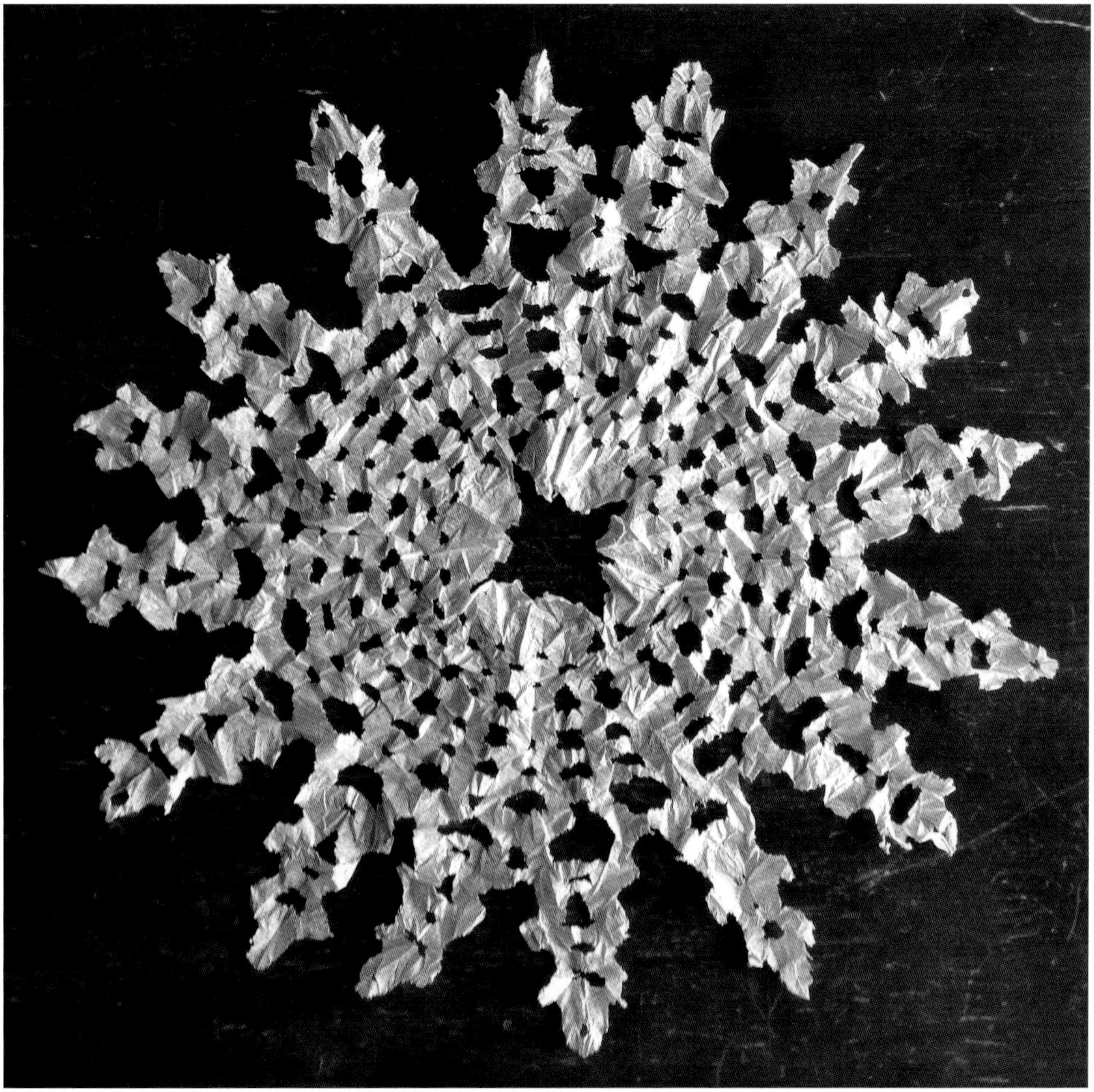

Snowflake 2
Brian D. Parker, 2014

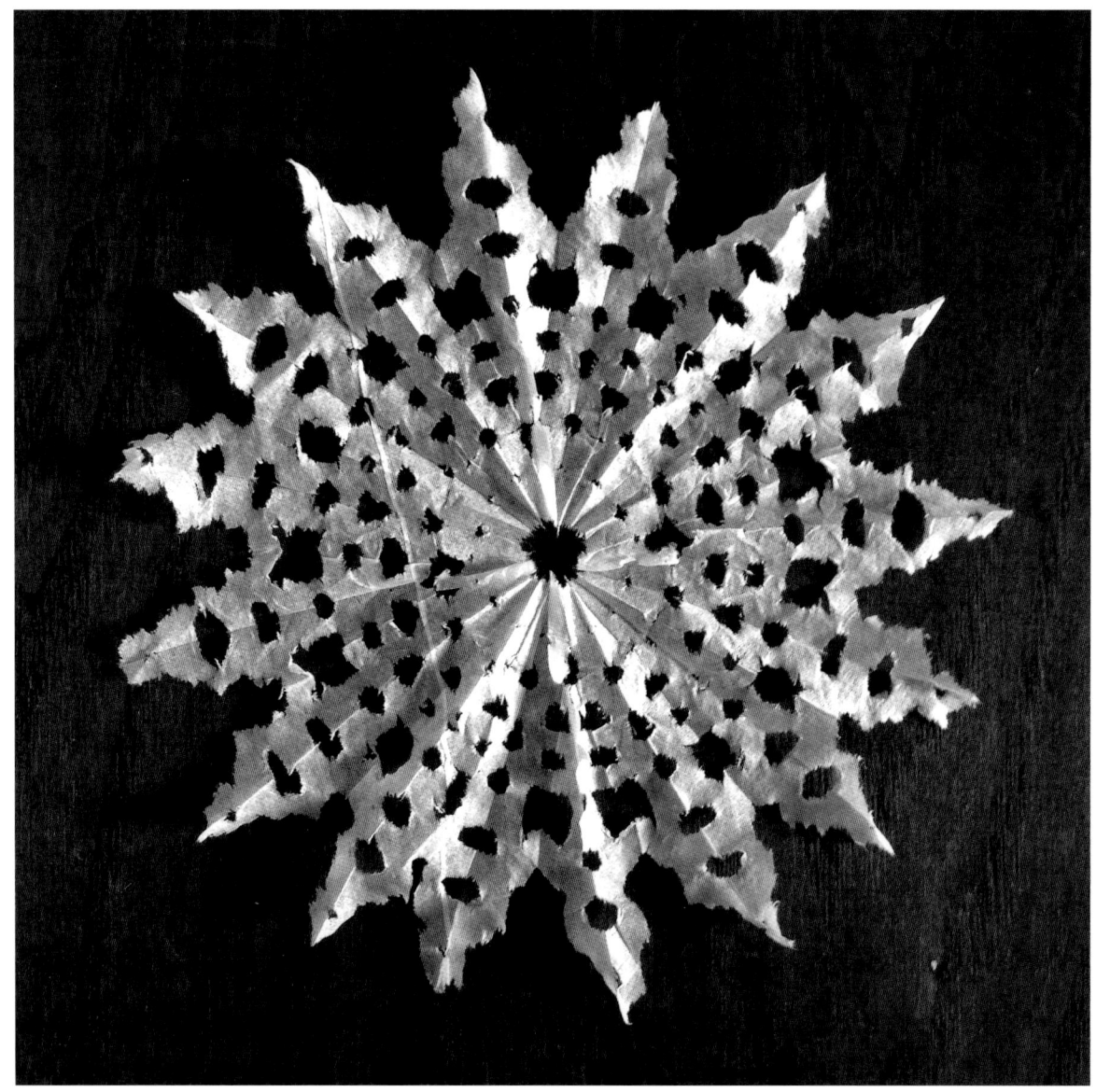

Snowflake 3
Brian D. Parker, 2014

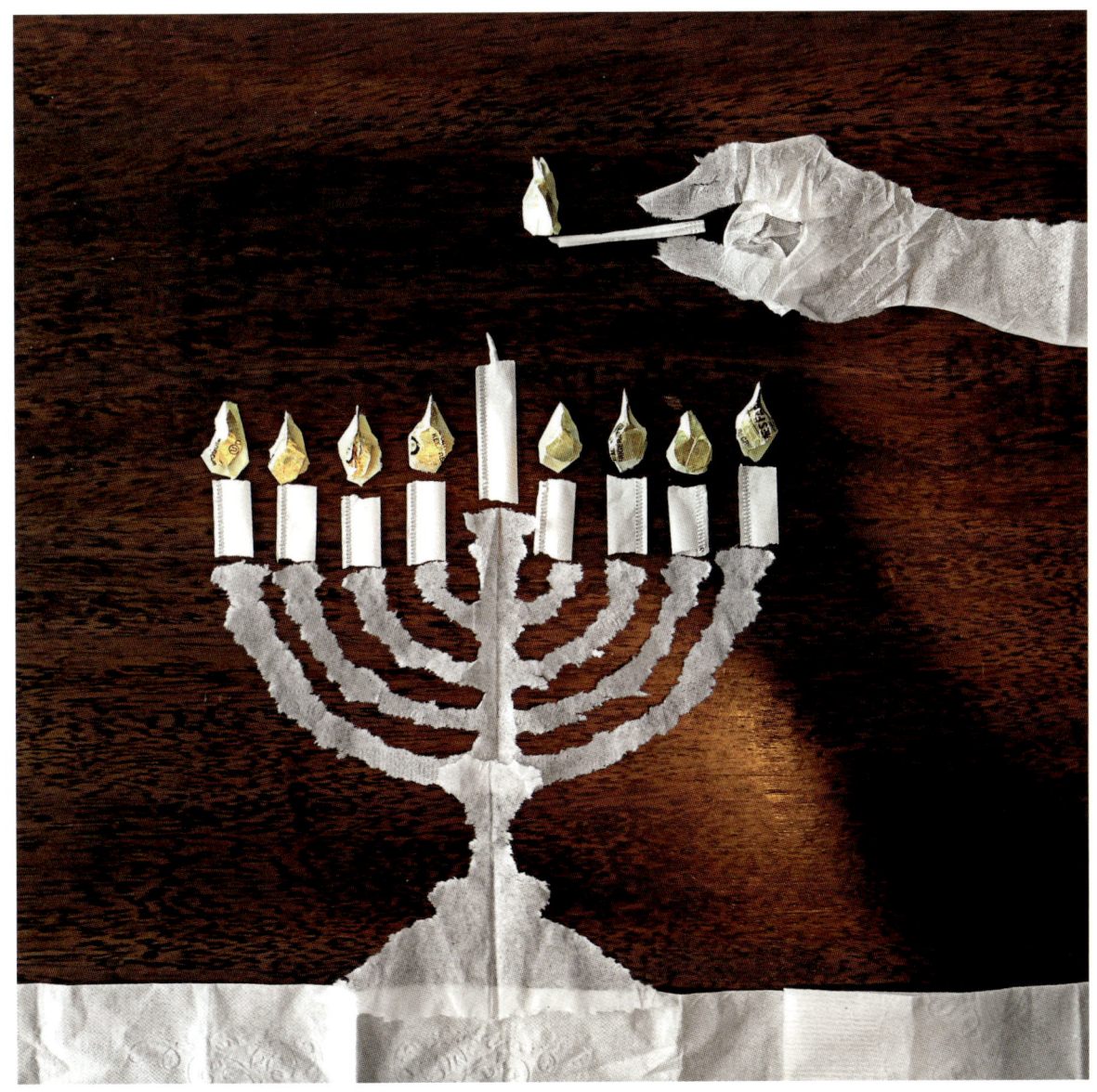

Menorah
Brian D. Parker, 2014

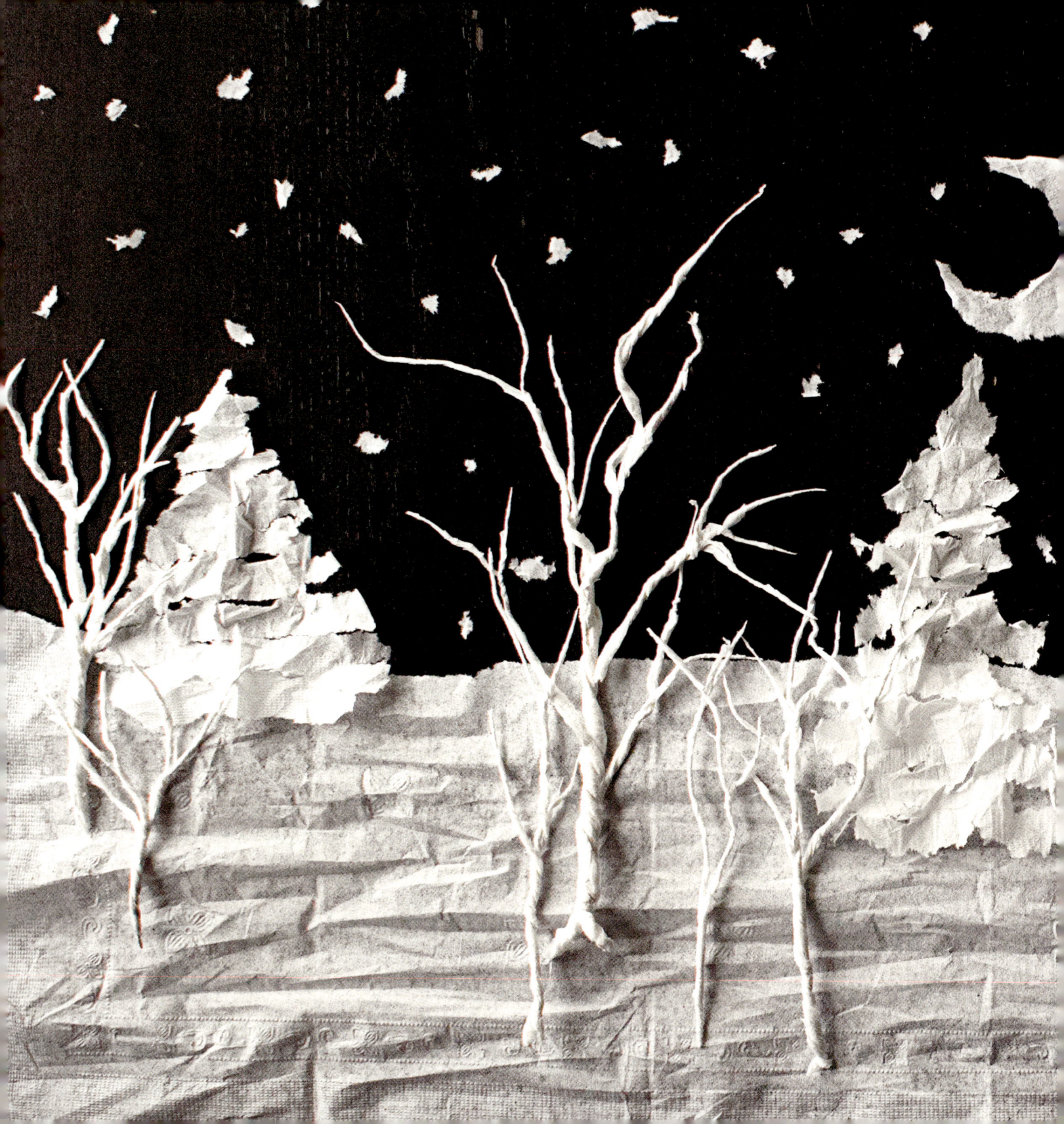

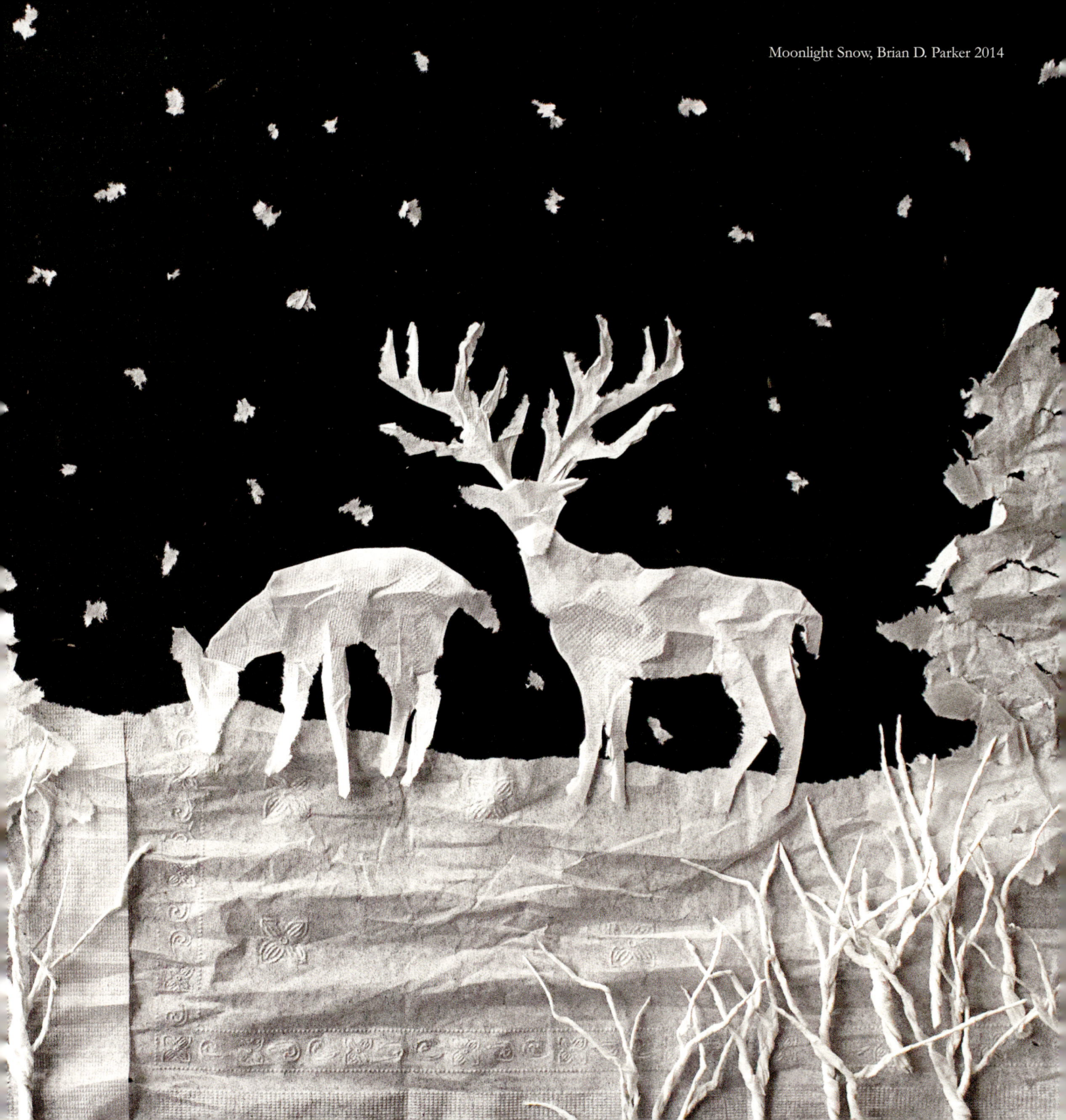

Moonlight Snow, Brian D. Parker 2014

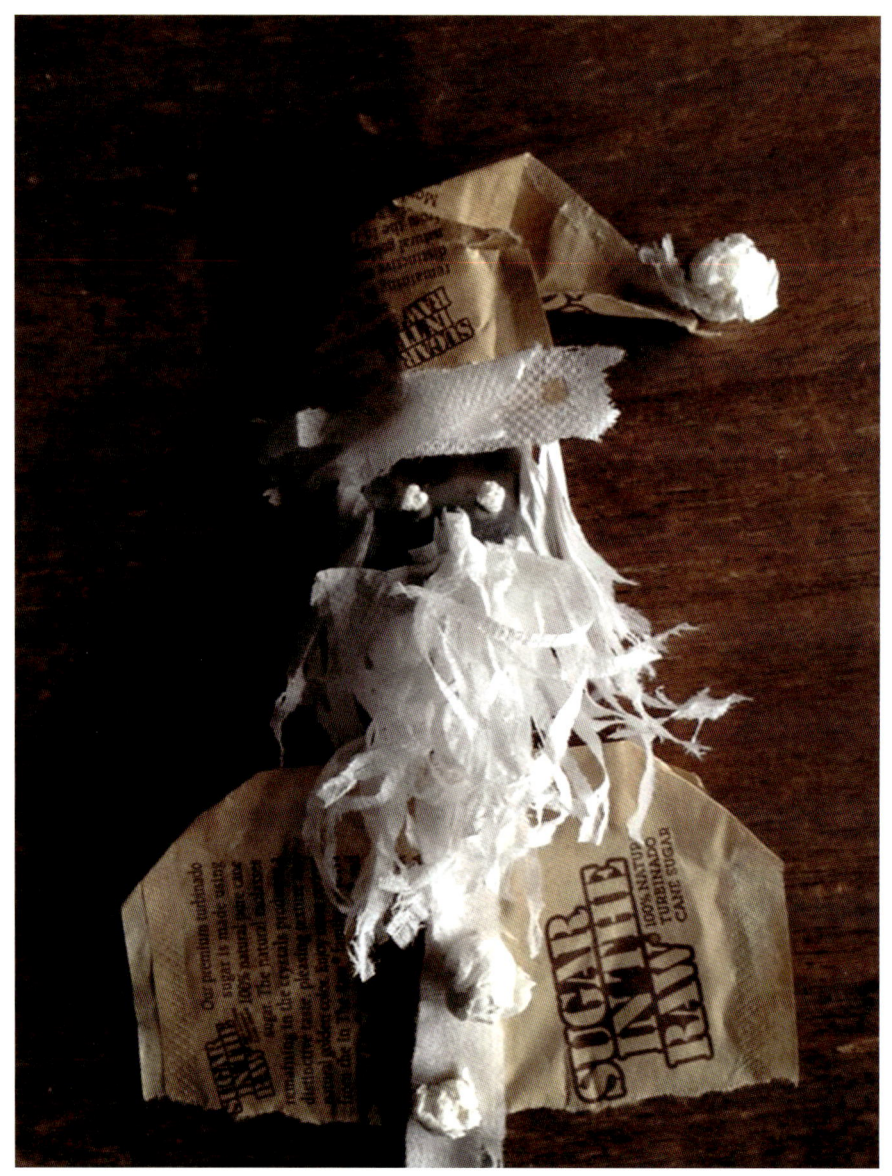

Father Christmas
Brian D. Parker, 2013

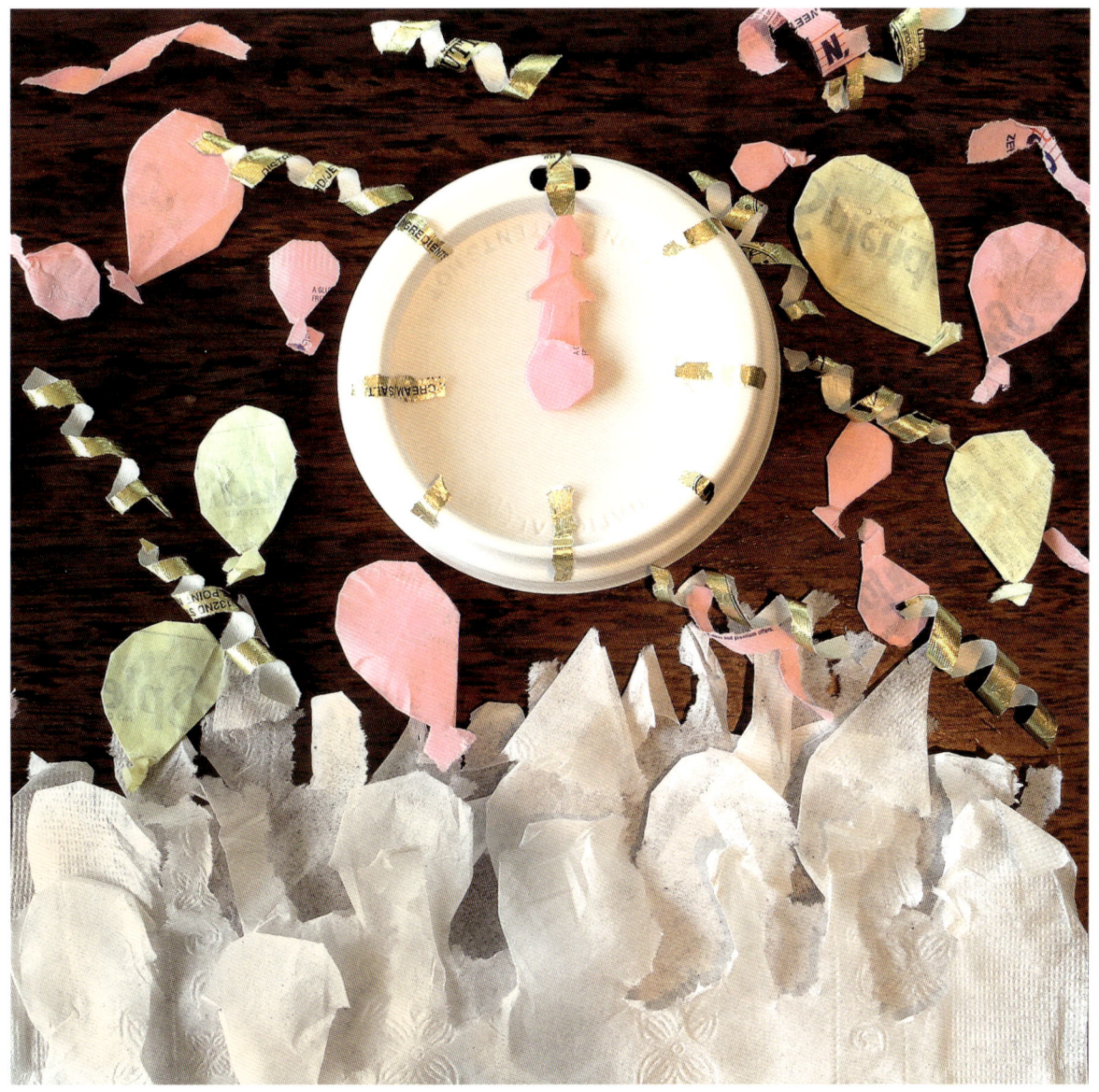

Happy New Year
Brian D. Parker, 2014

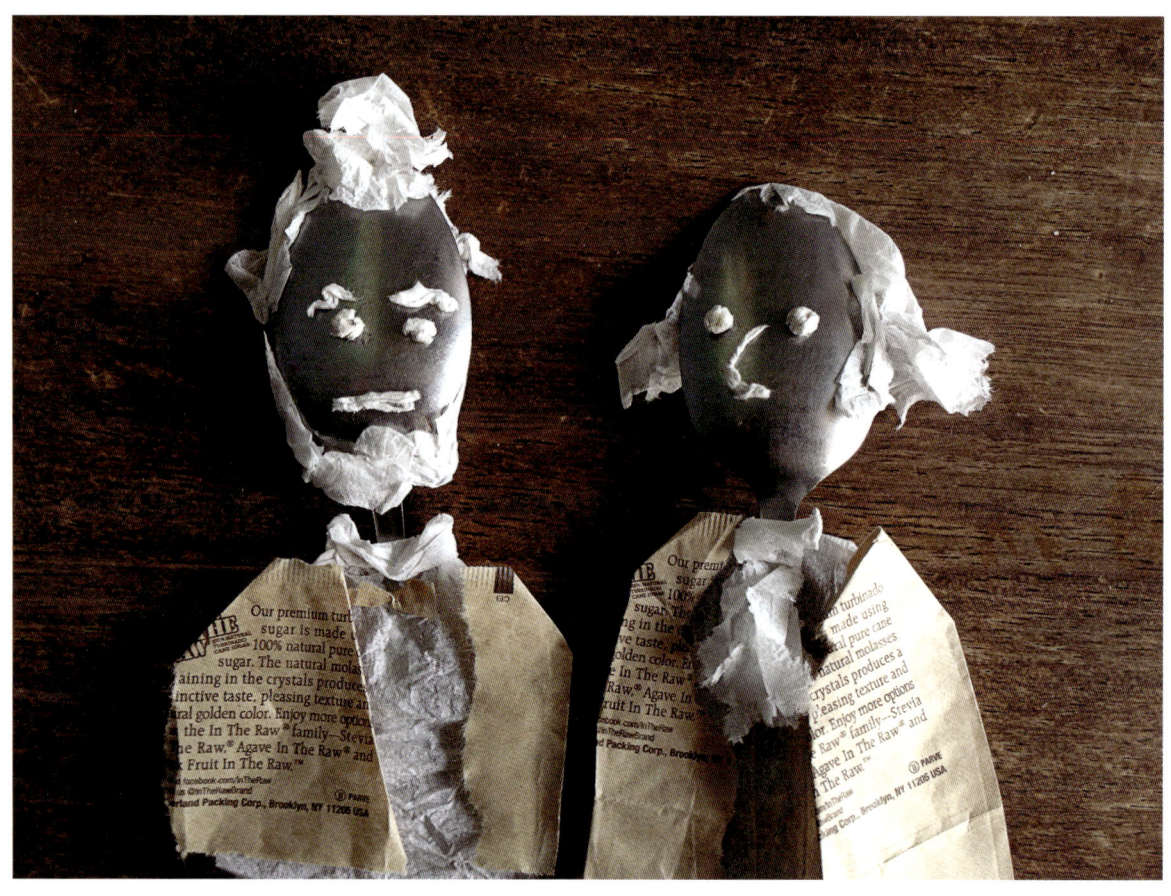

Presidents' Day
Brian D. Parker, 2014

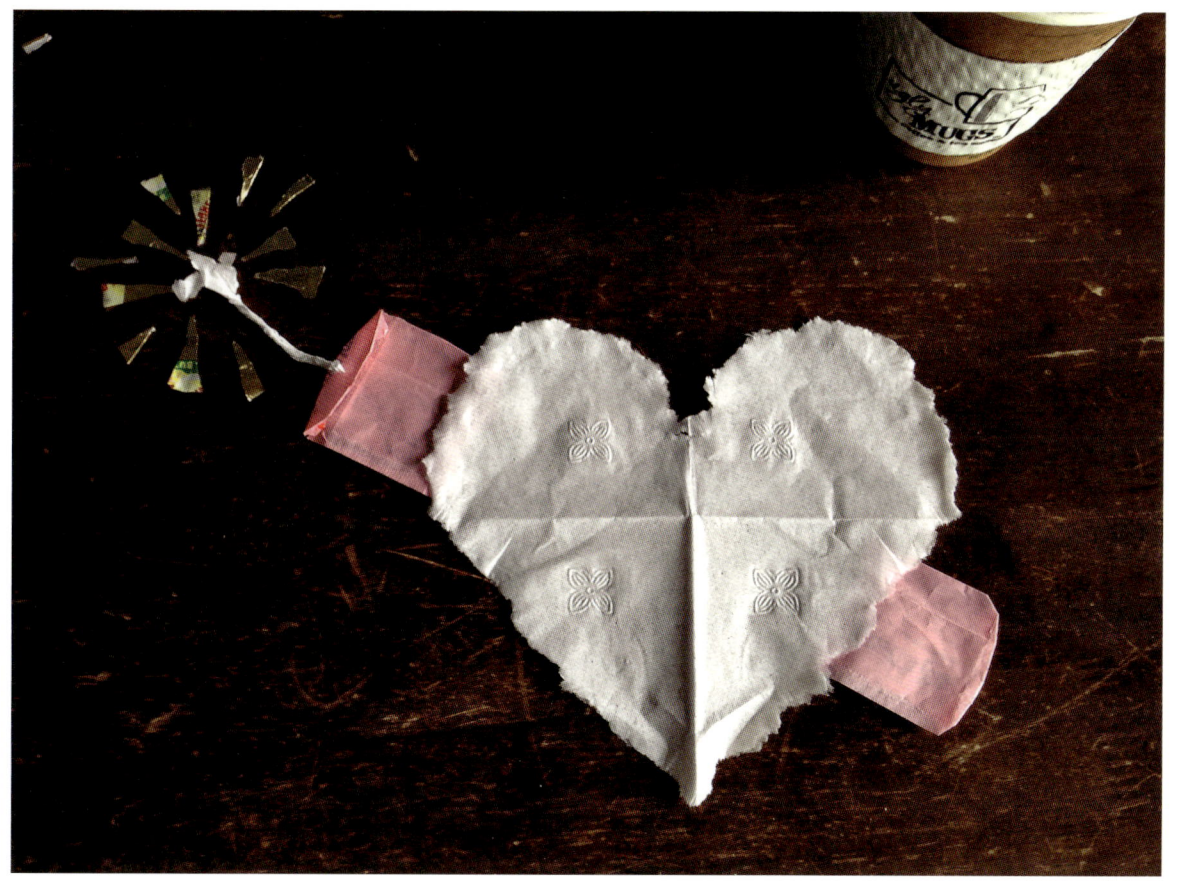

Valentine's Day
Brian D. Parker, 2014

AFTERWORD

All the spoons have been washed. The napkins have been recycled. You have seen the photographs, but the artwork is gone. Maybe it will come back as your grocery bag someday.

I have always connected with temporary art. And really, all art is temporary. Archive all you like, but in a thousand years the art will probably have joined us in the earth. I am preternaturally attracted to that cycle. I remember on childhood vacations watching my sand sculptures disappear in the tide. I didn't fight it. I didn't regret it even though I'd spent hours passionately extracting art from the beach.

It has been a lifelong habit, this making and disposing. I don't have anything against permanent art. I love it. I make it. I buy it. But I have always found great entertainment in creating quick disposable art with the random stuff of every day.

Barry and I went to an artist lecture by two professors from New England. They were brilliant, but one particular thing they said excited me. "We throw tons of our art away." What freedom! I wanted to go home and burn everything and start over. I remembered Georgia O'Keeffe and her willingness to prime over a painting, or let her art blow away in the wind. She wrote, "When I knew I was going to stay in New York, I sent for things I had left in Texas. They came in a barrel and among them were all my old drawings and paintings.

I put them in with the wastepaper trash to throw away and that night when Stieglitz and I came home after dark the paintings and drawings were blowing all over the street. We left them there and went in."*

Art is my life. And I don't imply that it should all be thrown away. I would love to see my permanent art in a museum. But temporary art is its own genre. The fact that it disappears is part of the experience.

While most of you weren't there for my experience, I want to thank you for sharing this part of the art adventure with me.

People often tell me that I should preserve the napkin art in a shadow box. I have done that on a couple of occasions. But there is just something about the throwing away that vibrates with me. I love the freedom and simplicity. For an hour or so I sip coffee, sculpt napkins, and then it is over. Next?

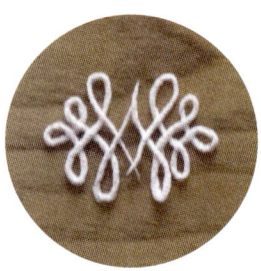

Georgia O'Keeffe by Georgia O'Keeffe. New York: Viking Press

THANK YOU

Much gratitude and joy and many, many blessings to you.

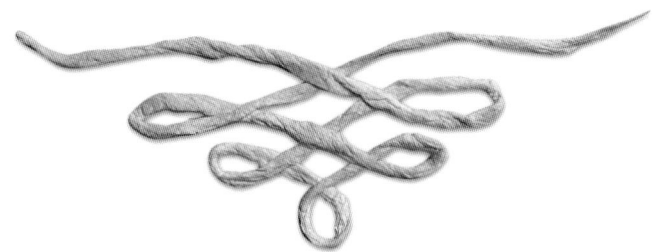

Steve Angus, Alana Bolan, Tom Brodhead, Shaun Brown, Dustin Burleson,
Chris and Annette Semanchin-Jones, Heather Calvin, Douglas Candano, Liz Carrier,
Josh & Heather Childs, Lantz Contreras, Vanessa Cole, Charlie Cox, Trish Crist,
Jarod & Courtney Delozier, Andrea Denney & Beth Reich, Kaaren Engel,
Holly Finale Finley, Kelly Fuller & Bob Thomas, Sonja Gibson, Laurens Glass, Phil Goins,
Henry Haggard & Evelyn Blythe, Laura Hardee, Mike Harley, Dan Heller, Robert Hiers,
Felix & Rebecca Hottenstein, Clay Humphrey, Scott Humston, Joni Jarnagin,
Kevin Johnson, Kem Schmalzer, Jonathan & Jocelyn Kasper, Emily Katzenstein,
Jon & Michelle Klavohn, Ken LeClair, Lori Mechem & Roger Spencer,
Kristine Mylls & Dudley Lightsey, Nashville Jazz Workshop, Diane Neighbors,
Jimmy & Tina Patterson, Omonpéé W. Petcoff, Winter Pope, Amy & Craig Clark,
Mitch & Angie Pryor, Gordon P. Publow, Jr., Ben Quick, Monica Ramey, Stephanie Reeves,
Kelly Anne Ross, Amy Sammartino, Bob Schatz, Don Schlosser, Kurt Schreiber,
Linda Smalley, Mike Smith, Steve Smith, Vangie Ruth Stahl, Don Stratton,
Allison & Billy Stroud, Cheryl Harris Sumida, Lisa Hillin Taylor, Suzan Toney,
Frank Trew, Nancy A. VanReece, Carol Westlake and Jody Bailey, Dorian Woodruff,
Henry Wrenn, Holly Yarbrough, Kyle Young

A SPECIAL THANK YOU

I share my pride, my appreciation and my happiness with you.

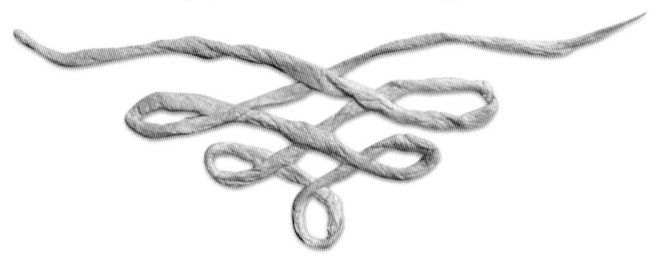

Jason Bradley	Keith Little
Iris Buhl	Kelli McCullough
Matt and Julia Coale	Robert B. Miller
Green Daniel	April Mullins
Titus Daniels	Gus Nagey
Emily Dillman	Clifton and Jennifer Ogden
Arvid Ekenberg	Lisa Ruble and Jim Graham
Amy Fair	Tama Powers Tappan
Graham and Adriana Gerdeman	Hunter and Carol Coppenger Whittington
Shawn and Melissa Frye Goodin	David and Lisa Wright
Garth Hawkins and Neal Appelbaum	John and Susan Zacharias

WITH DEEPEST GRATITUDE

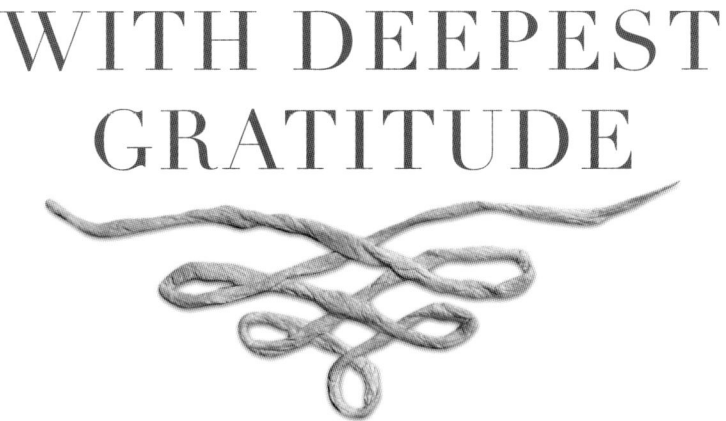

Barry A. Noland, Greg Page, Ian Hundt, Amelia Garretson-Persans, Kurt Schreiber, Neal Appelbaum, Kevin Johnson, Jason Parker, Jeremy Childs, Travis Cole, Andy Torres, F. Lynne Bachleda, Tama Tappan, Elyse Adler, Lori Mechem, Roger Spencer, Jarod Delozier and the fantastic crew at Ugly Mugs, Jason Bradley, John Hussey, Daniel Lewis and everyone at PK Pictures/NuMynd Studios, Billy Senese, Jonathan Richter.

I share with you my overwhelming gratitude. You have freely given your ideas, support, advice, enthusiasm and your expertise. You are brilliant, magnificent friends and champions. I tip my head low and thank you.

INDEX OF ARTWORK

*artwork with QR Code link to video

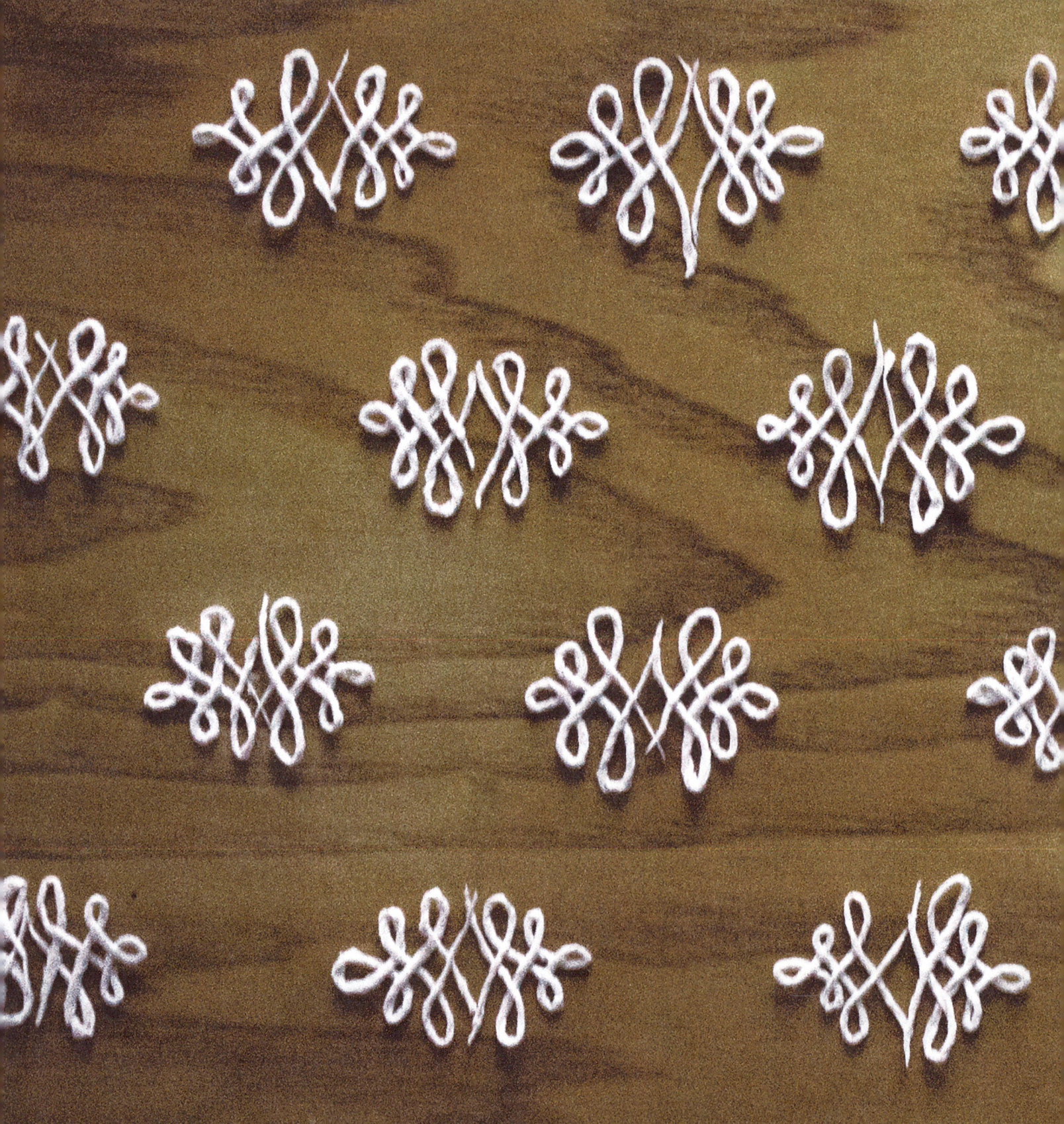